S. Hrg. 113–580

THE ROLE OF TRADE AND TECHNOLOGY IN 21ST-CENTURY MANUFACTURING

HEARING

BEFORE THE

COMMITTEE ON FINANCE
UNITED STATES SENATE

ONE HUNDRED THIRTEENTH CONGRESS

SECOND SESSION

JULY 17, 2014

Printed for the use of the Committee on Finance

U.S. GOVERNMENT PUBLISHING OFFICE

93–516—PDF   WASHINGTON : 2015

CONTENTS

OPENING STATEMENTS

WITNESSES

ALPHABETICAL LISTING AND APPENDIX MATERIAL

THE ROLE OF TRADE AND TECHNOLOGY IN 21ST-CENTURY MANUFACTURING

THURSDAY, JULY 17, 2014

U.S. SENATE,
COMMITTEE ON FINANCE,
Washington, DC.

The hearing was convened, pursuant to notice, at 10:06 a.m., in room SD–215, Dirksen Senate Office Building, Hon. Ron Wyden (chairman of the committee) presiding.

Present: Senators Cantwell, Cardin, Brown, Hatch, Grassley, Thune, and Isakson.

Also present: Democratic Staff: Joshua Sheinkman, Staff Director; Lisa Pearlman, International Trade Counsel; and Jayme White, Chief Advisor for International Competitiveness and Innovation. Republican Staff: Everett Eissenstat, Chief International Trade Counsel; Shane Warren, International Trade Counsel; Rebecca Eubank, International Trade Analyst; and Kevin Rosenbaum, Detailee.

OPENING STATEMENT OF HON. RON WYDEN, A U.S. SENATOR FROM OREGON, CHAIRMAN, COMMITTEE ON FINANCE

The CHAIRMAN. The Finance Committee will come to order.

Americans, from the water cooler to professional societies, now often debate the future of American manufacturing. Academic journals, for example, are filled with articles where naysayers say that American manufacturers cannot compete with cheap labor in Asia or that robots and computers do the jobs once held by our hardworking middle-class workers.

This hearing is going to show that it is too soon to hang the crepe on American manufacturing. There is genuine reason to be optimistic, because many American manufacturing companies—many American manufacturing companies—now succeed in tough global markets. Manufacturing accounts for more than $2 trillion in the American economy, it supports more than 17 million American jobs, and it drives three-quarters of all private sector spending on research and development. There are many more players in the manufacturing game worldwide, but the bottom line is, America is more than holding its own.

Now, that is not to say there have not been significant changes in recent years, and it is not to say that it is going to be exclusively smooth sailing from this point on. U.S. manufacturers have run up against greater competition today. Some of it is unfair, and 50 or 60 years ago the United States was the world's factory, accounting for 40 percent of the world's manufacturing goods. Today, the U.S. accounts for less than 20 percent.

Yet, American manufacturing has real strengths and opportunities to build on. For example, technology is an area where it is ''advantage America.'' The same is true in finished products and production methods. It is important for the Finance Committee to identify and examine which policies have stifled manufacturing and learn the lessons of the past. So the focus today is going to be on how to come up with fresh trade-related policies that can unleash the full potential of American manufacturers and give our manufacturers—American manufacturers—a new springboard to good-paying, middle-class jobs.

So there is a tremendous opportunity before American producers. There are going to be about a billion new middle-class consumers in markets around the world with significant sums of money to spend. That number is only going to grow as more people rise from poverty. Many of those consumers prize American products. They look for the American brand because the American brand represents top-notch quality, safety, and reliability. The American brand is a winner. Furthermore, American manufacturers are at the forefront of a number of fields, innovative fields, that are going to lead our economy in the future: clean energy, health care, and information technology are just a handful of examples.

For example, I am very pleased that Oregon's largest manufacturer, Intel, is here today. Their products are at the core of computing equipment and form the foundation of the global digital economy. Intel competes and they win in tough global markets. There are many more examples of vibrant manufacturers from Oregon and from other States.

Brammo, based just outside Medford, makes award-winning electric vehicles. A-dec, based in Newberg, makes some of the world's best dental equipment. Erickson, based in Portland, makes heavy-lift aircraft for a huge number of uses.

Now, I think I have established that American manufacturing has a lot of room to grow, and I think every member of this committee—we have Democrats and Republicans here—can also attest to the fact that in their home states there are thriving, cutting-edge manufacturers that are winning in tough global markets. The investments these manufacturers make support stable, healthy communities, and they create good-paying jobs for our hardworking middle class.

The bottom line? The right policies, especially on trade, can help launch a new era defined by successful, sustained manufacturing in America. Those policies ought to reflect what American manufacturing looks like today and where it is headed in the future, and not in effect be tethered to what was done 10 or 20 years ago. Our new policies have to dismantle trade barriers American manufacturers face abroad, like tariffs on high-tech products, requirements to relocate factories, intellectual property theft, and anti-competitive subsidies for state-owned enterprises.

New policies have to foster an environment in which American manufacturers of all sizes can grow and create good-paying middle-class jobs. The challenge ought to be, colleagues, to make things here, add value to them here, and then ship them, ship that American brand around the world.

Today's hearing gives the Finance Committee a chance to, on a bipartisan basis, develop those trade policies that can meet those objectives. Senator Hatch has been a close partner in all of these issues. For those of you who were not here yesterday, Senator Hatch made some extremely important points yesterday with respect to protecting American intellectual property.

[The prepared statement of Chairman Wyden appears in the appendix.]

The CHAIRMAN. Senator Hatch, we welcome your statement.

OPENING STATEMENT OF HON. ORRIN G. HATCH, A U.S. SENATOR FROM UTAH

Senator HATCH. Well, thank you very much, Mr. Chairman, for holding this hearing on the role of trade and technology in the 21st century with regard to manufacturing.

The success of our manufacturing sector is vital. Nearly 12 million Americans are directly employed by manufacturing. That is nearly 1 out of 10 American jobs. This is true in my State, where nearly 10 percent of working Utahans are employed in manufacturing. That is 120,000 jobs in Utah alone. That is one reason I am happy Ray Kimber is here with us today, and we welcome all three of you with us today.

I often talk about the small, innovative company that begins in a garage and grows to become the driver of economic growth and a source of jobs. That is Kimber Kable. Twenty-five years ago, Mr. Kimber figured out a way to weave audio cables to reduce unwanted noise and improve fidelity. He founded Kimber Kable to manufacture those cables, and now he employs 30 people in Ogden, UT. He sells his cables to the world. Today, two-thirds of Kimber Kables are shipped to customers overseas.

Ray is not only a friend, he is also an outstanding example of a larger truth, that the U.S. manufacturing sector is the most innovative in the world and American workers are unsurpassed in manufacturing productivity. Because of U.S. innovation and productivity, in those areas where U.S. manufacturing competes on an equal footing, it succeeds.

Our manufacturers maintain a trade surplus of $60 billion per year with the 20 countries where we have a free trade agreement in place. Per capita, the consumers from those countries purchased nearly 13 times more U.S. goods than consumers from the rest of the world. When you find a market that is open and secured by strong international trade rules, you will find goods like Mr. Kimber's that are manufactured in America.

Put simply, U.S. trade agreements are good for U.S. manufacturers, but we need to do a better job of opening overseas markets and making sure that our manufacturers do not face discrimination and other trade barriers. There are several negotiations under way with our partners in the Pacific region, in Europe, and in the World Trade Organization that will help address the challenges faced by U.S. manufacturers, but I do not think any of these efforts are going to succeed without Trade Promotion Authority, or TPA.

Without TPA, this administration is severely handicapped in negotiating high-quality agreements that will benefit American manufacturers and achieve the goals of Congress. That is why in January former Senator Baucus and I introduced the bipartisan Congressional Trade Priorities Act which would renew TPA and empower our trade negotiators to bring home trade agreements that meet the high standards set by Congress and to see those agreements passed into law.

Importantly, the bill sets negotiating objectives for our agreements. I want to highlight two of those today. We have witnesses with us here today representing companies that have created and taken advantage of advances in technology. Part of getting their products around the world happens to be digital trade. That is why the TPA bill we introduced requires U.S. trade agreements to ensure that electronically delivered goods and services are classified with the most liberal trade treatment possible and that our trading partners allow the free flow of data across borders.

But using the Internet to market, sell, and transmit digital products is only part of the story. These companies are also innovators, and their innovations must be protected. Our witnesses today have experienced first-hand the destructive impact of intellectual property theft. Mr. Kimber, for example, has had to contend with counterfeiters stealing his company's name to sell inferior products.

Our TPA bill also requires that U.S. trade agreements reflect a standard of intellectual property rights protection similar to that found in U.S. law, and it calls for an end to the theft of U.S. intellectual property by foreign governments, including piracy and the theft of trade secrets, and for the elimination of measures that require U.S. companies to locate their intellectual property abroad in return for market access.

For our manufacturers to continue to succeed overseas, we must also ensure our companies are able to exploit global supply chains so they can access the best inputs, add the most value to products, and ship their goods around the world as efficiently as possible. That is why last year former Senator Baucus and I introduced the Trade Facilitation and Trade Enforcement and Reauthorization Act to make trade facilitation a top priority at U.S. Customs and Border Protection and to improve intellectual property rights enforcement at the border.

Trade is good for U.S. manufacturing. Like I said, where our manufacturers operate in markets secured by free trade agreements, they succeed. But the challenges they face around the world are only growing, and we in Congress need to do our part to help achieve the conditions overseas under which American manufacturers can thrive.

That being the case, I hope the committee will soon be able to consider some of these pending trade bills. We really cannot afford to wait, and I want to personally express my regard for our chairman of this committee, who has worked very hard to try to work in a bipartisan way to get these things done, and who I think shares much of the same feelings that I do about international trade and what we need to do and how we need to do it. So I thank you, Mr. Chairman.

The CHAIRMAN. Thank you, Senator Hatch. I will not turn this into a bouquet-tossing contest, but I really appreciate the fact that, consistently, we are trying to work in a bipartisan way here in the Finance Committee. Certainly, as your statement indicated, manufacturing is an ideal opportunity for doing that.

[The prepared statement of Senator Hatch appears in the appendix.]

The CHAIRMAN. So we welcome our guests. First before us will be Mr. Stephen Ezell, who is a senior analyst at the Information Technology and Innovation Foundation.

Next will be Ms. Jacklyn Sturm, who is vice president and general manager of global supply management at Intel Corporation. They, of course, have an enormous footprint in my home State in manufacturing, and around the country. We are happy to have Ms. Sturm here.

Finally—and we already heard some glowing remarks, almost an introduction of Mr. Kimber—we are happy to have you, Mr. Kimber. He is the founder and owner of Kimber Kable, a manufacturer from Utah. Let the record show that Mr. Kimber's testimony is also going to be on behalf of another organization that we worked very closely with, the Consumer Electronics Association, and we always appreciate the input of that fine group.

So let us begin with Mr. Ezell. Welcome.

STATEMENT OF STEPHEN J. EZELL, SENIOR ANALYST, INFORMATION TECHNOLOGY AND INNOVATION FOUNDATION, WASHINGTON, DC

Mr. EZELL. Chairman Wyden, Ranking Member Hatch, and members of the committee, I appreciate the opportunity to discuss the role of trade and technology in 21st-century manufacturing and commend you for taking up this important topic.

Today I would like to provide an overview of America's manufacturing economy and offer several policy recommendations to bolster it. You have ably detailed manufacturing's vital importance to the U.S. economy. Unfortunately, the 2000s were a disaster for U.S. manufacturing, as America lost almost 6 million, or one-third, of its manufacturing jobs and saw real manufacturing output, when measured accurately, decline by 11 percent.

Yet today we hear talk of an inevitable U.S. manufacturing renaissance. For example, the Boston Consulting Group recently asserted that lower production costs will fuel a dramatic re-shoring of U.S. manufacturing, generating up to 5 million new jobs by 2020. To be sure, lower energy costs, a slightly depreciated dollar, and mostly rising foreign wages will help, yet the reality is that U.S. manufacturing costs per worker hour are already quite low, just 60 percent of Germany's level and only 20 percent higher than South Korea's.

Despite this, when one excludes the U.S. computer and electronic sector—because official government data overstates this sector's output—U.S. manufacturing value added in 2012 actually remained 7.4 percent below 2007 levels. America has fewer manufacturing factories today than it did just 2 years ago. While we have added back 650,000 manufacturing jobs since 2010, this only recovers one-tenth of the loss we experienced in the 2000s.

Likewise, while we have stemmed the outsourcing tide, at best we are at parity, with the United States re-shoring roughly one manufacturing job for each one off-shore today. In short, some believe that simply getting the business climate right and costs low enough are all that is needed for American manufacturing to thrive, but lower manufacturing costs alone will not restore the erosion of an industrial commons that has left America unable to manufacture a wide variety of high-technology products, nor will they address countries' rampant and growing use of innovation work-influenced trade practices which seek to advantage domestic producers at the expense of American manufacturers. These policies, which the World Trade Organization found countries used at an all-time record high in 2012, include currency manipulation, export subsidies, discriminatory technology standards, intellectual property theft, and localization barriers to trade which force American enterprises to manufacture locally or sacrifice intellectual property if they desire access to foreign markets.

Rather, it will require effective technology and trade policies to ensure that American manufacturers can reliably innovate and fairly compete in global markets. With one in three U.S. manufacturing jobs dependent on exports and more than 90 percent of the world's consumers living beyond America's shores, Congress should support market-expanding free trade agreements such as the TTIP, TPP, and an expanded Information Technology Agreement which could boost U.S. exports of information technology products by $3 billion annually, supporting 60,000 U.S. jobs.

With the U.S. Export-Import Bank supporting $37 billion in U.S. exports annually and 205,000 U.S. jobs in 2013, it is imperative that Congress swiftly renew the bank's authorization. Congress can also help boost exports by strengthening American manufacturers' ability to innovate next-generation products by expanding the research and development tax credit and supporting a national network for manufacturing innovation.

But innovative products will not reach foreign markets unless America commits to combating foreign mercantilism, thus Congress should require the U.S. Trade Representative's office to rank nations according to the extent of their use of mercantilist practices, while providing it with significantly expanded resources for trade enforcement.

In conclusion, American manufacturing can once again become a key driver of U.S. economic and employment growth, but that will not happen in the absence of constructive and comprehensive public policies to support American manufacturing competitiveness.

Thanks. I look forward to your questions.

The CHAIRMAN. Thank you very much, Mr. Ezell.

[The prepared statement of Mr. Ezell appears in the appendix.]

The CHAIRMAN. Ms. Sturm, welcome.

STATEMENT OF JACKLYN A. STURM, VICE PRESIDENT AND GENERAL MANAGER OF GLOBAL SUPPLY MANAGEMENT, INTEL CORPORATION, SANTA CLARA, CA

Ms. STURM. Good morning, Chairman Wyden, Ranking Member Hatch, and members of the committee. I appreciate the opportunity to discuss how increased trade can help strengthen 21st-century technology manufacturing.

Intel is a prime example of why the U.S. Government should open up new markets and remove existing trade barriers overseas to increase U.S. exports. Although we began as a small start-up, today Intel is the world's largest semiconductor manufacturer, and our products power everything from phones and tablets to servers and super-computers, and they form the foundation of the information economy.

Last year, the International Trade Commission reported that semiconductors were among the top three U.S. manufactured exports. Intel's revenue in 2013 was about $53 billion, and it was generated from sales to customers in more than 120 countries. In fact, more than three-fourths of our sales are actually generated outside of the U.S., yet, at the same time, three-fourths of our advanced manufacturing and R&D are conducted across 23 States here in the U.S. The revenue we generate selling domestically manufactured products outside this country helps create and sustain high-paying jobs here at home. Of our over 100,000 employees worldwide, more than half are based in the U.S. This domestically manufactured/internationally sold dynamic is fundamental to the growth of our business.

But our access to foreign markets does not just impact Intel and its employees. To support our business, we contract with over 7,000 suppliers in 46 States, and more than 3,000 of those suppliers are classified as small businesses. In 2012 alone, Intel's multiplier effect on the U.S. GDP was more than $96 billion.

All of these economic benefits, however, are dependent upon our ability to sell innovative semi-conductor products outside of the U.S., although they are made in the U.S., to the 95 percent of consumers who live overseas. So today I would like to make three key points to ensure that the U.S. Government trade agenda protects and promotes further U.S. manufacturing such as ours.

First, existing trade agreements need to be expanded. Too many key markets are subject to too few existing trade rules. One key example in our industry is the WTO Information Technology Agreement, which dramatically increased U.S. exports when it was implemented, by eliminating significant duties in many countries on a range of technology products. Unfortunately, many of the digital products developed in the last decade are not covered by the ITA, which was negotiated back in 1997. The Information Technology and Innovation Foundation estimates that expansion of ITA could increase direct U.S. exports by $2.8 billion, boost U.S. revenues by $10 billion, and support an increase of 60,000 new jobs.

Intel strongly supports the administration's efforts to expand product coverage of this aging agreement and, because of the accelerating pace of technology and innovation, it is imperative that ITA expansion be completed quickly.

Second, the U.S. must enter into additional robust trade agreements on an accelerated basis. America's 20 existing free trade agreement partners account for less than 10 percent of the global economy, but those 20 partners purchased nearly half of all of U.S. manufactured goods exported. U.S. exports create and sustain U.S. jobs. We need more FTAs to create more of those U.S. jobs.

We appreciate the administration's ongoing negotiations of both TTIP and TPP. TPP will set the standard for market access in the Asia Pacific region and, of most interest to Intel, USTR has pushed hard for language that will increase trade secret protection, enhance e-commerce provisions, restrict commercial encryption regulation, and ensure more robust due process protection in competition cases. We hope this agreement will be completed quickly, but without sacrificing quality.

TTIP is another key initiative. The transatlantic economy accounts for nearly half of the world's GDP and a third of its trade. When the U.S. and E.U. speak with one voice on emerging trade issues such as forced IP transfer and tech mandates, we set a precedent that other governments are more likely to follow. Despite these major agreements in the works, other economies such as Europe and India have entered more regional trade agreements than the U.S.

As global competitiveness increases, our pace to increase market access for U.S. goods and services must also increase. However, we should also ensure that our FTAs are robust and effective. If and when Congress considers Trade Promotion Authority, it should direct negotiators to fully address 21st-century manufacturing challenges.

Third, the government must use a variety of mechanisms to tackle ever more complex non-tariff barriers, or NTBs. Some governments are linking traditional NTBs, such as local content measures, with new NTBs that promote discriminatory standards and favor domestic intellectual property rights to create national manufacturing champions. Existing trade rules do not deal with these complex NTBs holistically, and new trade agreements are not likely to adequately fill the gaps or keep up with rapid technological developments.

For example, the government should seek other ways besides FTAs to isolate data protectionism, while dealing with legitimate privacy and security concerns, including development of best practices through increased international collaboration.

Finally, trade agreements should be living documents that can be easily updated to effectively address new barriers raised by greater global competitiveness in the information economy.

Intel appreciates the chance to share our views, and we look forward to working with you to ensure that trade agreements help American manufacturers prosper and create more jobs here at home. Thank you.

The CHAIRMAN. Ms. Sturm, thank you very much. We appreciate your comments and having Intel pay good wages to so many Oregonians day in and day out. We thank you.

[The prepared statement of Ms. Sturm appears in the appendix.]

The CHAIRMAN. Let us welcome Mr. Kimber.

STATEMENT OF RAY KIMBER, FOUNDER, OWNER, AND PRESIDENT, KIMBER KABLE, ON BEHALF OF KIMBER KABLE AND THE CONSUMER ELECTRONICS ASSOCIATION, OGDEN, UT

Mr. KIMBER. Good morning, Chairman Wyden, Ranking Member Hatch, and distinguished members of the committee. My name is Ray Kimber. I am founder and CEO of Kimber Kable of Ogden,

UT. It is my pleasure to appear today on behalf of Kimber Kable and the Consumer Electronics Association, of which I am a long-standing member.

CEA owns and produces the international Consumer Electronics Show, the global stage for innovation. CEA's over 2,000 member companies represent the $211-billion U.S. consumer electronics industry, and that is an updated figure from just yesterday.

I founded my company in 1979 with the Kimber Kable product line of audio, video, and speaker cables. Over time, our innovations have established us as a global leader in sound technology and audio cable. Our product improves the fidelity of entire audio/video systems. Both Kimber Kable and CEA rely upon an open global marketplace with policies that promote free trade and protect our innovations at home and abroad.

Kimber Kable employs 30 people in Ogden, UT, where our product is manufactured in a facility one and a half times the size of a football field. Approximately 60 to 70 percent of the product we manufacture in Utah is exported to nearly 60 countries. Kimber Kable is typical of U.S. manufacturers that rely on access to international markets for continued growth and success. Enactment of trade agreements and legislation which protect us against counterfeiters and trademark infringers are strong examples of areas where my government can help me and other American innovators.

I commend you, Mr. Chairman and Ranking Member, for working with industry to secure agreements and policies that U.S. companies need to be competitive. Free trade agreements have worked for us in the past. FTAs increase confidence and certainty for U.S. industry doing business in those partner countries.

America's free trade agreement partner countries buy more goods from the U.S. than other countries. We want new FTAs negotiated and passed by Congress to establish good rules where U.S. companies can operate with confidence that they have protections and enforcement. Please do not forget counterfeiting, an area in which we face daily challenges and damages. Agreements currently under negotiation, such as the Trans-Atlantic Trade and Investment Partnership and the Trade in Services Agreement, can do just that.

For agreements to be concluded swiftly, we need FTA partners to trust that the United States has the ability to actually pass these agreements into law. Trade Promotion Authority expired in 2007, and, without its renewal, we risk that negotiated trade agreements will never pass into law. That costs me, my employees, and our families in Utah, along with the entire U.S. economy. It literally diminishes our ability to innovate and remain competitive in the global marketplace.

Finally, I want to address a pending agreement, the success of which would be a boon to our industry. The Information Technology Agreement, ITA, was negotiated over 15 years ago and has not been updated since. Products such as video games and consoles and the audio/video systems that support them are not part of the original agreement.

Updating the ITA to include these will make them more affordable, promoting greater production, thereby creating jobs. CEA and its members have been working tirelessly with the USTR to advance the deal. We could use Congress's help to encourage China to return to the negotiation table motivated to make significant and meaningful progress.

We risk falling behind other countries that are passing agreements with each other. How can you expect me to maintain innovative competitiveness if my government is not matching my passion with crucial agreements and legislation? I think a unified Congress which promptly passes needed agreements and bills will send just as strong a message as the content of the bills and agreements themselves. I respectfully say ''please.''

Thank you again for the opportunity to testify. I will sincerely respond to any questions that the committee may have.

The CHAIRMAN. Thank you all. You have been very, very helpful. I know you are going to get important questions from colleagues.

[The prepared statement of Mr. Kimber appears in the appendix.]

The CHAIRMAN. Let me start with you, Ms. Sturm, on the question of strengthening trade secret protection. It really is hard to over-emphasize the importance here, because we are talking about ''advantage America.'' These are our inventions. These are the creative efforts of Americans. Then you have threats from traditional moles and state-supported cyber-theft, a whole host of very significant efforts that are coming from around the world, that undermine our intellectual property.

I think it would be very helpful if Intel could start by outlining what the company sees as the major gaps—the major gaps today—in global trade secret protection.

Ms. STURM. Thank you, Mr. Chairman. Yes, we think trade secrets are critical to how we operate our business. We develop very advanced manufacturing techniques, and those are not patented because we do not even want them to be visible to the world. It is crucial to us that we protect them and that we maintain a high degree of confidentiality internally.

From the standpoint of trade secret capability, we would like to see more focus on enforcement and then also on better written trade agreements in the future that set up effective protections for trade secrets.

The CHAIRMAN. I also understand that, in the area of the trade secret rules, it seems that the rules are particularly weak in the area of these flimsy protections, on providing unfair advantages to state-owned enterprises, and with inadequate disciplines on technical standards. I understand that you all are concerned about those as well.

Ms. STURM. We look at those as non-tariff barriers. We certainly are concerned when preferential access is given to products that are inferior to ours. Relative to trade secrets, those protections really are in the realm of enforcing existing trade agreements and ensuring that future agreements build in even stronger protections.

The CHAIRMAN. Let me offer a question for you, Mr. Ezell. Senator Cantwell has done very good work on this question of the Export-Import Bank and is an eloquent advocate for it. I hear Oregonians talk a lot about how important it is for the small firms, that the small firms often just kind of get lost in this debate about great titans of enterprise, taking one position or another. You all work a lot with the small firms. What would be some examples of how the Export-Import Bank is important for the small firms?

Mr. EZELL. Well, regarding the question on the Export-Import Bank, I think it is first important to recognize that global export credit competition has only increased. In fact, over the past 5 years China and Germany respectively have issued 4 and 5 times as much export credit as the United States has, so we need to both reauthorize the Export Bank and increase its lending portfolio.

Now, with regard to the question of small and medium enterprises, the reality is that the vast majority of the bank's transactions—80 percent—go to SMEs. In 2013, the U.S. Export-Import Bank supported the export activities of 3,400 U.S. SMEs, so it can play a vital role in helping our small businesses export.

One other key point here, I think, is that sometimes you will hear the criticism of the Export-Import Bank that its activities only support the activities of larger corporations such as GE or Boeing. But the reality is that every single time the U.S. Export-Import Bank supports the sale of a Boeing aircraft, it is also supporting the activities of the 22,000 suppliers, the vast majority of them small businesses, that comprise Boeing's value chain for the production of aircraft. So across the board, from the bank support for large businesses to small ones, there are at heart supporting the export capacity of small U.S. businesses.

The CHAIRMAN. One last question if I might, for you, Mr. Ezell, and you, Mr. Kimber. When we are talking about the new priorities—because that is a big part of our agenda here, to respond to trade barriers—it seems to me that if we are dealing with preferences for a country's state-owned enterprises, requirements that U.S. companies produce in a foreign country to access its market, and these technical kinds of standards, these strike me as three of the areas that we really ought to zero in on. I think Ms. Sturm touched on those as well. Do you share that view, Mr. Kimber, and then Mr. Ezell?

Mr. KIMBER. I do. We have some markets—for instance, Brazil—where the import tariff for our class of goods is so high that it makes it untenable to even attempt much of a business down there. They do not have anybody that competes with us down there, so I do not really understand that.

What we have found is that, when we go into a market, it actually triggers and encourages legitimate competitors of our product for the benefit of the entire global marketplace. So I think that the high tariffs for products as collateral damage actually damage the country that establishes such high tariffs. So we can actually do them a favor by making them do the right thing.

The CHAIRMAN. You are being too logical, Mr. Kimber.

Mr. KIMBER. I am sorry.

The CHAIRMAN. It is an important point. We do not have too much of that in government.

Do you want to add anything, Mr. Ezell? I know my time is up.

Mr. EZELL. Just to say that the evolution of trade in the global economy is that, as countries have reduced their tariffs to trade, they have surreptitiously replaced them with these types of non-tariff barriers. I think you correctly called out localization barriers to trade that force U.S. companies to either locate their production offshore or to sacrifice their intellectual property as a condition of exporting to foreign markets as one of the key challenges we face.

For example, India recently put in place a policy called the Preferential Market Access policy which would have required that 80 percent of the computer and electronics sold in India by 2020 be manufactured there. While they have repealed that to only apply to government procurement of electronic products, these types of policies are poised to do significant damage to the global production system and also to U.S. manufacturers. You are exactly right to call on Congress to push back more strongly against them.

The CHAIRMAN. Very good.

Senator Hatch?

Senator HATCH. Well, thank you, Mr. Chairman.

Mr. Kimber, you export to almost 60 countries around the world, and, in many of these markets, your products still face high tariff barriers. I agree with you that updating the Information Technology Agreement would help you and other companies across the United States access growing foreign markets.

Can you give us some idea of what concluding an updated Information Technology Agreement would mean to your company and its ability to export to more countries, including China?

Mr. KIMBER. Yes. We actually export a fair amount to China now, but our biggest scourge is counterfeit products. Counterfeiting literally costs us. It deprives and deceives the consumers. Counterfeiting damages my reputation.

Let me show you how we struggle to grow and retain our overseas markets. These percentages are the export portion of our total sales: in 2012, we exported 76 percent; in 2013, 67 percent; in 2014 year-to-date, 62 percent. This sales erosion is directly tied to certain models of our product.

In countries around the globe like Taiwan, China, Canada, even right here in the U.S., counterfeit goods are running roughshod, damaging both manufacturers and consumers. Sometimes it even seems that counterfeit producers are aided, or at least protected, by local governments.

Senator Hatch, I believe that your efforts to introduce the Customs reauthorization bill will have a measurable benefit to me and to the CEA members and the U.S. economy, if passed. This bill would direct agencies to coordinate with each other and with Kimber Kable. We need to stop bad product crossing the border. Current Customs and Border Protection internal policies impede such cooperation and coordination. This is an action that CEA members have long urged.

It is illogical to continue CBP's internal policy that impedes cooperation and coordination. Legislation such as the proposed Customs reauthorization bill will streamline information sharing and is a critical action that Congress should take to protect all consumers and help domestic manufacturers like me. Please pass this bill. Thank you.

Senator HATCH. Thanks, Mr. Kimber.

Ms. Sturm, you pointed out in your statement that trade secret theft is a growing problem around the world. We know that China in particular is systematically stealing critical information from hundreds of U.S. companies. That is why the Trade Promotion Authority bill that we introduced earlier this year includes provisions directed at combating this threat, including new provisions calling for governments to protect trade secret information and to prevent or eliminate their involvement in the theft of trade secrets. So would you please tell us why it is so important for our trade agreements to address this growing threat?

Ms. STURM. Advanced manufacturing requires an effective use of trade secrets to deliver high-yield, low-cost products, and protecting those trade secrets allows companies to stay competitive. At this point, we believe that our trade secrets are well-protected inside our company, but we believe that trade agreements need to be better enforced to ensure that individuals and countries that do not follow these agreements are penalized and that the penalties are effective enough to make an impact on those countries.

Senator HATCH. Thank you.

Mr. Ezell, ITIF published a report in April of 2014 entitled, ''The Indian Economy at the Crossroads.'' In that report, you make a compelling case that the path to growing India's economy lies in India repudiating its ''innovation mercantilist'' policies of the past and instead embracing an economic model that respects intellectual property rights, attracts investment, and of course unleashes India's labor productivity.

Now, we are all hopeful that India's new Prime Minister Modi will follow that path. Unfortunately, I understand that one of the first trade actions by the new Indian government at the World Trade Organization was to block consensus on a protocol to implement the trade facilitation agreement. I find that very troubling.

What can we do as a government to help make the case that policies that protect intellectual property, enhance trade facilitation, and liberalize trade and investment, are key tools to economic development?

Mr. EZELL. I think several things. The first will be to demonstrate that policies such as local content requirements, which mandate our companies to locate production in these nations, are not as effective as these countries focusing on providing an attractive and compelling location for our manufacturers to put their production activities there.

For example, Intel would certainly not put a semiconductor fabrication facility in India where there are rolling blackouts, so it is incumbent upon us to show them that investing in the innovation potential and the infrastructure in their own economy is what they need to attract the manufacturing activity that can drive their growth.

I think it is also important to point out that, when you look at intellectual property in India, for example, a lot of the people who are most strongly damaged by intellectual property theft are content creators, for example, in Bollywood, which is the second-largest movie production industry in the world. IP theft of movies and digital content affects their own innovators. So when India does not implement as strong an intellectual property rights statute as it could, it only damages the long-term innovation potential of its own economy. Having a whole-government approach that constantly makes that case toward Indian colleagues, I think, is one of the strongest things we can do to get them to put in place strong intellectual property rights statutes and better trade rules.

Senator HATCH. Thank you, Mr. Chairman.

The CHAIRMAN. Thank you, Senator Hatch.

Senator Brown?

Senator BROWN. Thank you, Mr. Chairman.

Recently—and this question is for you, Ms. Sturm—DOJ indicted five Chinese military officers for the cyber-theft of trade secrets from U.S. manufacturers and the United Steelworkers. The stealing of trade secrets by the Chinese military underscores just how valuable IP and trade secrets of U.S. manufacturers are to the Chinese government. We know, or we think, that there has been a long-term pattern of that kind of abuse of the rule of law.

I met earlier this week with the Software Alliance and talked about some of these issues on trade secrets and theft of trade secrets. Is this threat one of the reasons that Intel and other companies you observe are looking to in-source, to bring jobs back here?

Ms. STURM. Like most major companies, Intel is subject to cyber-attacks with the intent to extract IP. We do not think it is isolated to China at all. Relative to our operations, we think that we have robust controls that protect us from that, so, no.

Senator BROWN. All right.

It is pretty apparent, it is pretty obvious, that U.S. trade policy and tax policy have encouraged jobs, American companies, to relocate overseas. It is pretty interesting. The last 20 years is the only time period I can think of in economic history around the world where companies will shut down in Cleveland and move production to Wuhan and then sell their products back to Ohio, or back to Cleveland, or back to the United States, and it has become a business plan for a number of U.S. companies.

There are other factors of course, but trade agreements and tax policy seem to have played into that. What happens is we, the most innovative country probably in the history of the world, with a great system of research and development and universities, we lead the world in innovation still. But when the production goes overseas, both in terms of process and product, the innovation takes place on the shop floor, making a production more efficient and making a product itself that is manufactured better.

What do we change about U.S. trade policy? What does TPP do, what does TTIP do, to begin to change that whole view that is part of many companies' business plans: to shut down here, move overseas, and sell back into the United States? How do we change trade policy, tax policy? This is for both Mr. Ezell and Ms. Sturm. How does that play with these proposed trade agreements, and what do you suggest we do to encourage companies to no longer do that and to begin to re-shore jobs?

Ms. STURM. I think the most important thing that could be done to affect those kinds of changes is comprehensive tax reform. In particular, in the short-term, a stronger and permanent R&D tax credit would stimulate companies to retain a lot of those activities at home.

Senator BROWN. Mr. Ezell?

Mr. EZELL. So ITIF talks about the four Ts, which we call Technology, Trade, Tax, and Talent policy. I think countries have to get that suite of policies right to create an attractive environment in which manufacturing can occur. With regard to tax policy, for example, U.S. manufacturers pay a corporate tax rate that is 37-percent higher than Asian manufacturers do, so we do need a corporate tax reform.

However, in the process of doing that, we should not sacrifice incentives for firms to invest in research and development and investment. For example, the U.S. only has the world's 27th most generous R&D tax credit now. Brazil, China, and India even offer more attractive R&D tax credits than we do, so we need to increase our incentives for American firms to invest in innovation and capital equipment.

Senator BROWN. So is this going to just be a continued race to see which countries can have the lowest tax rates? I mean, you see that the chairman has shown great leadership when dealing with this inversion issue. The chase just continues. We do not have the highest effective tax rates in the world.

I mean, I think there is a bit of disingenuousness in somebody always saying, from the *Wall Street Journal* and other people all the time, we have the highest tax rates in the world. Well, look at effective tax rates. I think we need change. I am not arguing against that. But where does this end?

I mean, you live in this country, you work in this country. You benefit from infrastructure, you benefit from medical research, you benefit in your businesses, let alone personally, from scientific research. You benefit in the freedoms we have. Then you want to move just to continue to lobby for and look for the lowest tax rates. We are just going to keep moving and keep moving and keep moving. Is that where we end up? Mr. Kimber?

Mr. KIMBER. Well, I would make the point that the actual tax rate is not as important or crucial to me as the complexity of how to assure that I pay the right tax. I view the complexity of how much time, effort, and money we spend on outside professionals to make sure that even we, as a small company, pay the correct amount as the essential equivalent of a non-tariff barrier.

If you could make it more certain, less complex, I think that would help. I do not mind paying taxes. I understand the benefits, and I support appropriate taxation. But to have it so convoluted that it makes it difficult for me to be assured that I am paying the right amount, that kind of uncertainty is something you guys could fix, and I wish you would, please.

Senator BROWN. I think Senators Wyden and Hatch have argued for a simpler tax system. We will have other decisions to make with it, but I think there is general agreement on that.

Mr. KIMBER. So, thank you.

Senator BROWN. Would the two of you like to comment on my question?

Ms. STURM. Yes. Let me say that we are looking for a level playing field. As we go around the world, countries come to us repeatedly looking to bring our high-skilled, high-paying jobs into their country. They routinely offer us a billion or more dollars, which is largely comprised of tax-based incentives, to bring those jobs, to operate in their countries. So that does create an uneven playing field, and that is one of the issues that we would like to see addressed.

Senator BROWN. Mr. Ezell?

Mr. EZELL. I would stress, on tax policy, that it is about assessing where we stand competitively via other countries. It is also about ensuring that more of those tax dollars go back into reinvesting in the manufacturing capabilities of our firms. For example, we have a great program called the U.S. Manufacturing Extension Partnership, which supports the innovation capacity of small businesses. When you look at countries like Germany, they invest 3 times as much as a share of GDP as we do, Japan 20 times as much. So reinvesting those tax dollars in our innovation potential, I think, is very important.

Senator BROWN. Fair enough. Thank you. Thank you.

The CHAIRMAN. Thank you, Senator Brown.

Before we go to Senator Isakson, I want to address a number of the important points that Senator Brown made. What Senator Brown was talking about is how we grow red, white, and blue jobs, jobs in this country—high-skill, high-wage jobs for our people, this point that Senator Brown touched on with respect to innovation taking place on the factory floor. We just want to make sure that those factory floors are in the United States. So what Senator Hatch and I and all our colleagues have tried to do on a bipartisan basis is attack those kinds of opportunities to do it.

For example, a number of you mentioned the research and development tax credit. That is in the extenders package, not just the way it used to be, but as an improved version so as to do more to create opportunities for inventors, as Senator Brown so correctly said—to have the innovation on the factory floors here in America.

Also, colleagues, so we know, because we have had several references to the matter of the international taxation debate, next Tuesday we will have an extremely important hearing on international taxes that will touch on, obviously first and foremost, the inversion question. Senator Hatch and I are working with colleagues to tackle that in a bipartisan way as well.

Senator Isakson?

Senator ISAKSON. Mr. Chairman, I am going to apologize for not asking a question, but there is no need to really ask a question of these three witnesses. Our only problem today is, they had the wrong audience. We ought to send these remarks to the leadership of the Senate in both parties to make them realize that we have a lot of work to do. Ms. Cantwell is going to talk about the Export-Import Bank. I think she is going to sing out of Mr. Ezell's hymnal about the importance of that.

I am going to talk about what Ms. Sturm said on the TPA. I mean, Trade Promotion Authority is absolutely essential if we are ever going to do a TTIP or a Trans-Pacific Partnership. We have the African Growth and Opportunity Act, which I know we have a hearing coming up on.

The biggest enemy of manufacturing domestically in the United States of America is the U.S. House and Senate. We need to pass the legislation that facilitates the ability for them to do business.

I will add one other statement that was not mentioned, and that is the Miscellaneous Tariff bill. There are a lot of 20th-century manufacturers in the United States still producing a lot of jobs who make products that have components in them that are minute in their import value but have heavy tariffs on them that cost the American manufacturer a lot of money.

This committee should be moving forward on the Miscellaneous Tariff bill, moving forward on the two partnership bills. But understand that nothing is going to happen without us taking action on the Export-Import Bank, TPP, AGOA, TTIP, and Trade Promotion Authority. I want to commend the witnesses on addressing the key points of what we need to pay attention to as members of the U.S. Senate.

Thank you very much.

The CHAIRMAN. Well said, Senator Isakson.

Next is Senator Cantwell, the leader of the effort on the Export-Import Bank, and particularly on raising that question of the small companies.

Senator CANTWELL. Thank you, Mr. Chairman. I want to associate my comments with the member from Georgia, because I think Senator Isakson hit the nail right on the head. You guys have clearly outlined what we need to be doing, and we here need to do our job.

I think so many people think that we are somehow helping U.S. manufacturing when all we are doing is delaying the certainty and predictability that they need to compete. They have to focus every single day on shipping product. That is the level of competition that they face. They are so busy focusing on shipping product, yet we think they should take time away from that competition and come and run around the halls here and explain to us in intimate detail things that we cannot understand. I would rather they be competitive and ship their product and have us do our job.

So first of all, I want to thank you, Mr. Ezell, for clearly articulating that the health of U.S. manufacturing depends on exports. I do not think we can emphasize that enough, that the market is outside the United States of America.

I have a question, though. Your testimony—I am trying to understand the upside and the down-side in manufacturing. So I think you are saying—well, let me try this. We used to have about 18 million manufacturing jobs in the United States?

Mr. EZELL. That is correct.

Senator CANTWELL. All right. And we lost 6 million, so we are down to about 12 or 13?

Mr. EZELL. Twelve-point-one million, yes.

Senator CANTWELL. All right. So we are at 12 million. All right. What is the upside for us and what is the risk side? By that I mean, how big of an upside do you think we have in manufacturing? I am not asking for an exact, precise number, but I know in aviation, we have a world demand for 35,000 new airplanes. That is a lot of jobs. But we have to build them, we have to compete, we have to have the Export-Import Bank to sell them, all of that. So what do you think the upside is for the U.S. economy on manufacturing, if we proceed correctly?

Mr. EZELL. I think the upside is at least 3 to 5 million more U.S. manufacturing jobs. The key point of my testimony was that we cannot rely on market forces and lower production costs alone,

18

though they are important. But they will not be sufficient to ensure a U.S. manufacturing renaissance without these types of proactive public policies around trade and technology that we have been talking about here today.

One key point I would just like to make——

Senator CANTWELL. Well, our calling card in the competitive arena is our ability to innovate, correct? Our ability to innovate next-generation faster than anybody else, right?

Mr. EZELL. That is precisely right.

Senator CANTWELL. All right.

Mr. EZELL. And our ability to do so depends on three conditions existing in global marketplaces. First is the existence of large markets, because our innovative products, like aircraft and semiconductors, have very high fixed costs of initial design and development, so their marginal costs need to be spread across larger global markets. That does not happen when other countries are closed to our exports. Intellectual property theft then becomes a key threat to our ability to innovate, because so much of our innovation is knowledge- and resource-intensive.

Then when you get excess competition in the global economy—for example, India recently issued a compulsory license for Bayer's Nexavar, an anti-cancer drug, and that is going to allow an Indian manufacturer to now produce a generic copy.

So it creates excess competition in the global economy which prevents our manufacturers not only from competing, but from then generating profits from one generation of innovation that can be reinvested into the future.

So, getting no excess competition, access to large markets, and protection of intellectual property rights in the global economy, are the key things we have to have to assure American innovation.

Senator CANTWELL. Well, I appreciate your speed there. Thank you. But what is the down-side? Because we are at 12 million, and if the upside is another 3.5 million or higher, what is the down-side if we do not act? What happens to that 12 million?

Mr. EZELL. Well, when you consider that we lost a third of our manufacturing jobs in the prior decade, if we do not get our act right, we could lose at least 20 to 30 percent in the coming decade. That is not inevitable. It should not happen. It does not have to happen.

But just very briefly, if you look back to the year 1997, the U.S. has lost 43 percent of its manufacturing jobs when correcting for labor force growth; Germany has only lost 8 percent over that time. So Germany has put in place a right set of policies to support the export economy. We need to be thoughtful about looking at what other countries are doing smartly and how we can emulate such policies in the United States.

Senator CANTWELL. I do not know where else we can be so accountable for an upside of 3.5 million or a loss of 3.5 million. So, I mean, to me, as I said, I think my colleague Senator Isakson got it right.

I did want to just put up two charts quickly. To your earlier point, this is the U.S. aerospace supply chain. You can see that it has companies in every State in the United States. In fact, we are passing out for our colleagues today data and information about the supply chain companies that exist in their area. Then the second chart is just the actual Ex-Im larger supply chain, which is 33,000 companies. It shows by State each of those States and where these manufacturing jobs are.

So there is a lot at stake all throughout the United States. I do not think people—I noticed when I handed Senator Schumer his handout yesterday, he was delighted to see that there were more supply chain manufacturers in his State than in mine. So I think that you can see that it is all across the United States of America, and this is why we have to get this policy right. This is why we have to move forward on the Ex-Im Bank and these other policies we have discussed here today. So, thank you.

Mr. KIMBER. If I could just make note, even though our primary product is consumer electronics, we do supply component parts to the manufacturers for both aerospace and automotive. So internally we innovate these little ideas, and it has picked up, so it ends up being little parts inside of big parts that end up flying or driving.

Senator CANTWELL. If I could just, Mr. Chairman, make one last point. I think our colleagues just really need to understand what Mr. Kimber just said. Our competitive advantage is that the small companies are continuing to perfect the innovation, so it is flat organizations continuing to be the best experts at their particular area. That is why we can innovate faster, but it is a very spread-across-the-United States thing. So just because you do not hear from them does not mean they do not exist and they are not producing great products. We have to empower them.

Ms. STURM. If I may make one last comment relative to the downside. I agree with Mr. Ezell that there is a meaningful down-side, but I want to express that our international competitors are not standing still. So we may have experienced something from 1997 until now, but competition is accelerating, and, as preferential policies are being established by international governments, they are facilitating even greater acceleration there. So we must act.

The CHAIRMAN. I think the point Senator Cantwell makes very much dovetails with that last comment, Ms. Sturm. The reason Senator Cantwell pushes so hard for us to innovate and for policies that encourage that innovation is because of what you just said. We know the international competition is not just sitting around reading paperbacks; they are out there innovating, and we appreciate that.

Senator Thune has joined us, and we welcome him.

Senator THUNE. Thank you, Mr. Chairman, to you and Senator Hatch, for holding this hearing today. I want to thank our witnesses for being here.

I think many Americans would be surprised to know that the majority of our Nation's exports are manufactured goods. While many manufacturers face pressure from foreign competitors, the fact is that trade agreements, when they are enforced, make our trading partners play by the rules. I think that has been very successful in encouraging U.S. exports.

So, if you look at the countries around the world with which we do business, those with which we have free trade agreements, they constitute a big part of our manufactured exports. I think something we need to continue to do is aggressively expand those trading relationships through trade agreements. We need a renewed and strengthened TPA in order to do that. So let me put my plug in, as I am sure some of my colleagues, including Senator Hatch, have already done.

Ms. Sturm, I would like to ask a question about what you see in terms of the increasing trend of trading partners using non-tariff barriers as a way to block access to markets and unfairly block the flow of trade. What are the emerging trade barriers for IT goods and services?

We see a lot of those when we talk about agricultural exports, and that is something that I am a little bit more familiar with. But what areas, when it comes to the goods and services that a company like yours exports, what types of non-tariff barriers do you run into?

Ms. STURM. Thank you, Senator. What we see is preferential focus, and Mr. Ezell discussed the PMA in India, where governments are attempting to set preferential standards for locally developed technologies. Then those are implemented to the exclusion of other technology that may in fact be better, and this can limit the ability to bring leading-edge product to market.

Also, as Mr. Ezell pointed out, because of the scale of operations that are required in our high fixed-cost businesses, in order for us to be successful we need to be able to sell our product in very high volume. As countries limit our access to those markets through discriminatory standards or even through technology mandates, it reduces our ability to be competitive with our products, both from a cost standpoint as well as an access standpoint.

Senator THUNE. Mr. Kimber, there is a perception that exporting is generally something done only by multinational companies, and your company has 29 employees, yet you export the majority of what you manufacture to nearly 60 countries around the world, I understand.

So what particular challenges does a smaller company like yours face in becoming an exporter, and is there anything that Congress can do to make that process easier?

Mr. KIMBER. Well, the trade agreements, so that the tariffs are equalized and intellectual property rights are protected, are really key. For instance, we had a case where we had a serious inquiry from Vietnam years ago, and, because we sell parts to our own competitors, what they did not realize was, when they called in to one of our divisions to buy our own brand-name printed-on parts that they wanted to buy from us to put on counterfeit goods, that they were busted.

So, if we would have had a trade agreement with Vietnam at the time, I think that we would have stood a much better chance of being in that country legitimately, and so it has kind of a follow-on.

If I could draw a parallel between the type of development and research that we do, along with bringing an actual product to market, with the legislative product, it has to be the same way. If we design and just continue to re-design and re-design and never bring a product to market, then we do not ever know what we are doing, and we will get eaten alive by our competitors. So, I think that that is a fair analogy between development of legislative agreements and development of actual technology and products.

Senator THUNE. In your estimation, is this problem of counterfeit goods getting better or worse?

Mr. KIMBER. It is getting worse. We pay a lot of money to counsel just to take care of eBay. It is just like Whac-A-Mole. We can identify and we can figure it out, but it is tough. It is not just that they are competing with a product that mimics our technology; they are actually using our own brand name and our own trade dress.

Senator THUNE. Are there additional steps you think that we ought to be taking?

Mr. KIMBER. Yes. I think Senator Hatch's bill, where it requires, say, Border Patrol, the Customs people, to actually, if there is a product coming into the States that says Kimber Kable on it, contact us and say, we do not think this is yours, because we think that all of your product is made in the U.S. So we can put a stop to that right there. If we can impede that, it means we discourage it. If you discourage bad behavior long enough, hopefully it goes away.

Senator THUNE. Yes.

Mr. Chairman, my time has expired. Thank you. Thank you all very much.

The CHAIRMAN. Thank you, Senator Thune.

We have been joined by Senator Cardin. He is always ready to swing into action. Let us recognize him at this time.

Senator CARDIN. Well, Mr. Chairman, thank you. I want to thank our witnesses. I apologize for not being here for the full hearing. We had a Foreign Relations Committee meeting on the border issues. But I am extremely interested in this subject. I have been doing in Maryland what I call ''Made in Maryland'' tours and have really seen the innovation and creativity of manufacturing in our State.

I usually ask the people there what we can do to try to help. It is interesting. International trade comes up frequently, and I am talking about, as Senator Thune was mentioning, smaller companies. This past week I went to the Tulkoff company, which is the largest horseradish producer in the United States. It does not have much penetration outside the United States. Part of that is the type of products they manufacture, but part of it is the difficulty of a small company dealing with market access outside of the United States.

It seems to me that we have made a huge error in manufacturing in that we have sort of adopted the World Trade Organization's tax regime, which allows for consumption taxes to be border-adjusted, whereas we rely more on income taxes, which are not border-adjusted. When we tried to correct that, we got into trouble with the WTO, and the manufacturing credit has not really solved the problem.

So can you just share with me your thoughts on what would be the most important steps for us to take to try to help market access to smaller companies in manufacturing that produce products? What would be on top of your wish list if we could make certain changes to gain greater access for our companies in the international market? What is number-one on your list? What would you like to see? Don't be bashful—go. Mr. Ezell, why don't you start?

Mr. EZELL. Well, of course I would say that market access, expanding free trade agreements that can do a better job of opening global markets to our exporters, would be the first thing. But getting down to a more detailed and technical level, I think one thing that would really help is, I mentioned earlier our Manufacturing Extension Partnership, which is a program that helps our manufacturers innovate and adopt modern manufacturing processes.

But when you compare how that program operates in most other countries of the world, like Britain's Manufacturing and Advisory Service, they have an export orientation to that program where they are helping those small manufacturers understand needs and tastes in foreign markets, so they are helping them tailor their products and services to the taste of a global economy.

I think we can look at having MEP most certainly bolster the export potential of our small firms, and also have our embassies around the world be more attuned to the export capacity of our small manufacturers and make that a greater part of the trade portfolio at the embassy level.

Senator CARDIN. There have been some success stories in my State. Marlin Steel, which is a small steel manufacturer, exports a lot more than—I mean, the export market is huge for them even though they are a small specialty steel operation. So it has worked. I am not trying to say it cannot.

But it seems to me it is challenging for small manufacturers to take the risk of needing market share outside of the United States in order to be able to be successful. It seems to me that most of the initiatives that you are talking about are aimed more towards the larger manufacturers.

Mr. EZELL. Well, for example, the Manufacturing Extension Partnership is designed specifically for companies of less than 500 employees, so it is specifically targeted to SMEs. So, I think it could have an incremental impact, because the first order of business in getting to exports is that our manufacturers innovate next-generation products. So, I think it would play an important role.

Another point to elaborate on, one Mr. Kimber made earlier, is that small businesses are often subject to foreign firms counterfeiting or exploiting their intellectual property, and they clearly do not have the resources to contest those unfair trade practices, so we really do need to increase funding for agencies like the Interagency Trade Enforcement Committee, ITEC. The Senate legislation has called for $12 million in funding for this agency in 2015, the House only $7 million. We have to adequately resource these agencies.

Senator CARDIN. I agree completely. Also, we should have quality trade agreements that give us a better chance for manufacturing, quality trade agreements that have strong enforcement provisions for anti-competitive manufacturing practices in other countries, which we have been somewhat weak about.

Mr. KIMBER. Yes. Let me brag about a fellow CEA member. MiTek manufactures speakers in Ennis, TX. They have about 150 employees there. They also manufacture in Kentucky and Phoenix with about 100 employees each. They recently outfitted the Shanghai airport and the Shenzhen ferry station with U.S.-made paging systems, even in the face of a 40-percent tariff.

Can you imagine how good those products are to overcome that kind of price barrier? Imagine how much more innovation and how much more sales we would get if that trade tariff was even-handed on both sides. So it is important. We are overcoming it, and we can see how the technology can do it, but it is——

Senator CARDIN. Well, I agree with you. My time has expired, but let me just point out that in TPP one of the major issues is whether we really will get a level playing field on government procurement and state-owned enterprises, particularly in the developing countries that are aspirants in TPP.

So I agree with you on your trade, but there have to be quality agreements. The trade regime has been more skewed towards Europe and Asia from the point of view of their practices than it has through the United States, particularly on taxes but also on intellectual property. I look forward to working with you.

Thank you, Mr. Chairman.

Mr. KIMBER. Thank you, Senator.

The CHAIRMAN. Senator Cardin, well said. The ultimate compliment, I think, is Senator Hatch's, because he wanted me to mention specifically that he very much wanted to be here for your questions, and apparently he was called away by a scheduleing conflict. So as usual, you have made points that resonate here in a bipartisan way.

Senator CARDIN. Can I get a transcript of the exchange and give it to Senator Hatch?

The CHAIRMAN. Yes. I will make sure that that is available. I thank you for those valuable points. You know we are going to work very closely with you and your office on these questions in the context of these trade agreements.

The second thing I want to do, Mr. Kimber, is, I am very glad that now, on several occasions, you mentioned how important it is for the Congress to require the Customs agents to take the steps necessary to identify counterfeit goods. As you know, this is a problem around the country, but it is a big, big problem, as Ms. Sturm knows, in the Pacific Northwest. We are talking about fake computer chips, we are talking about fake Nikes, we are taking about all manner of fakes. So I am very glad that you have made that point. It is one that Senator Hatch and I will be following up on in a bipartisan way.

I have one last question that somehow we managed to not get at, and I think it would be good for you, Mr. Ezell, and any of you, if you choose, can comment on it.

Mr. Ezell, you in effect tried to kind of take us through some lessons to be learned from successful exporting industries. You really cited several that you felt were winning in global markets. Electronics, aerospace, pharmaceuticals, I think, were three that you cited.

Almost as a wrap-up and the fact that you all have done a lot of research, are there some broader policy lessons to be learned from the fact that there are some sectors that are doing well, some comments you can give about why they are doing well and perhaps policies that would allow us to get more sectors into what I call the winner's circle?

Mr. EZELL. I think today's most innovative companies recognize that there has been a globalization of both innovation production and innovation consumption. That means that these companies tap into global markets to find best-of-breed suppliers and partners, and they have the ability to export their finished products at scale to the entire world.

Another key point is that they embrace modern concepts of open and collaborative innovation. If you look at Proctor and Gamble, it gets 50 percent of its ideas for new products outside the company and beyond the shores. But you cannot have open innovation without open trade. This increasingly pernicious use of localization barriers to trade, which are both affecting manufacturing and digital markets, is a huge problem.

Indonesia and Vietnam, for example, recently announced localization barriers to digital trade that will require Internet companies to use local data centers in the provision of digital services. But, when you start to shut down cross-border data flows with these types of local data storage or local IT facility use requirements, then you are disrupting the global production and value chains on which modern innovation relies.

So, from a trade policy perspective, I think we need to ensure that our companies both have access to suppliers and partners across the world in modern global value chains and then also the ability to innovate their products on a global basis.

The CHAIRMAN. Thank all three of you. I am just going to send you off with one comment. I think you have reinforced again why those who are hanging crepe over the American manufacturing sector are just wrong. I talked, I think a couple of hours ago, about the American brand. It is really now, based on your testimony, the American manufacturing brand. We have a brand in the manufacturing sector that the world is interested in.

What I am taking away from your testimony today is that the two areas that we have really, I think, come back to again repeatedly—one of them is trade and one of them is tax—are both areas under the jurisdiction of the Finance Committee.

In effect, our big challenge is that policies in both of these areas really have not kept up with the times. You look, for example, at the tax issue. I have 9 years of sweat equity into the only bipartisan Federal income tax reform bills that have been put in front of the Senate in several decades. When you look at the 1986 tax reform debate, the global economy was hugely different in 1986.

Now it plays a much bigger role. And that is why it is so important in this set of hearings that we are really starting on Tues- day—where we will look at the global economy, where we will look at inversions—that we do it in a bipartisan way, that we recognize that, as I would describe it, we have a big job in the sense of playing catch-up ball so that the good work that you are doing, the innovation that you all are producing on your factory floors and in the areas that we have talked about, are not held back by policies in the tax area that are out of date.

On the trade issue, I often tell my colleagues—and lots of them were not even around for the TPA vote in 2002, which I supported—the times are very different. I remember as a young member of the House, having a full head of hair and rugged good looks back then—yes, Mr. Kimber—the President had the ex-Presidents to the White House. He talked for 45 minutes without notes, really kind of laying out what was then the challenge of exporting and getting American goods and services into global markets.

The digital economy was not a big factor in those early debates in the Clinton days. Now Senator Thune and I have a bipartisan piece of legislation to kind of update what we are doing on an issue that really was not even on the radar back then during those first years when President Clinton was inspiring a lot of us to really look to the future and figure out how to address it.

Now, as you have heard from my colleagues, I thought Senator Brown and Senator Cardin made some very important points about areas where we need, on a bipartisan basis, to update our trade laws. I just so appreciate the three of you. You have given us very helpful and thoughtful comments today, ones that I think we can pick up in this committee, particularly on the trade issue but also on the tax issue, in a bipartisan way. You can expect that we will be calling on you all often.

With that, the Finance Committee is adjourned.

[Whereupon, at 11:36 a.m., the hearing was concluded.]

A P P E N D I X

ADDITIONAL MATERIAL SUBMITTED FOR THE RECORD

Written Statement of

Stephen J. Ezell

Senior Analyst

Information Technology and Innovation Foundation

The Role of Trade and Technology in 21st-Century Manufacturing

before the

Committee on Finance

United States Senate

July 17, 2014

Chairman Wyden, Ranking Member Hatch, and members of the Committee, I appreciate the opportunity to discuss the role of trade and technology in 21st-century manufacturing and commend your Committee for taking up this important topic. Today, I would like to provide an overview of the past, present, and future of America's manufacturing economy and then offer several policy recommendations designed to bolster American manufacturing competitiveness.

Manufacturing matters immensely to the U.S. economy. Manufacturing contributes over $2.08 trillion to America's economy annually while directly supporting over 12.1 million high-wage U.S. jobs.[1] When indirect jobs are counted, manufacturing supports an estimated 17.4 million jobs in the United States— or about one in six private-sector jobs.[2] Manufacturing jobs, on average, pay 9 percent more in wages and benefits than jobs in the overall economy. One of the reasons jobs in manufacturing pay more is because manufacturing produces more exports, and exports contribute an additional 18 percent to workers' earnings on average in the U.S. manufacturing sector. Manufacturing also generates greater employment and economic spillovers than other sectors of the economy. For example, research finds that for every job created in manufacturing, as many as 2.5 jobs are created in other sectors of the economy, while an estimated additional $1.40 in output from other sectors is generated for every $1.00 in final sales of manufactured products.[3]

Yet manufacturing is also America's principal source of exports (i.e. traded sector competitiveness), research and development (R&D), and innovation activity, not to mention a key contributor to national security.[4] Manufacturing accounts for 57 percent of America's exports. In fact, perhaps the most important reason why manufacturing matters is that it's simply impossible to have a vibrant national economy without a globally competitive traded sector (those sectors that compete in international markets and whose output is sold, at least in part, to non-residents of the nation), and manufacturing is by far America's most important traded sector. Manufacturing is also a key driver of R&D and innovation in the U.S. economy. In fact, America's manufacturing sector accounts for 72 percent of all private sector R&D spending and employs 63 percent of domestic scientists and engineers. Moreover, U.S. manufacturing firms demonstrate almost three times the rate of innovation as U.S. services firms.[5]

Unfortunately, despite manufacturing's vital importance to the U.S. economy, the 2000s were a disaster for U.S. manufacturing, as America lost one-third of its manufacturing jobs—almost 6 million—a rate of job loss worse even than that experienced during the Great Depression.[6] While some have attributed these deep losses to increased manufacturing productivity, the reality is that U.S. manufacturing productivity grew at similar rates between 1990 and 1999 and between 2000 and 2009—56 percent and 61 percent, respectively—yet manufacturing employment declined just 3 percent in the former decade but 33 percent in the latter.[7] And while some argue that manufacturing is in decline across virtually all advanced economies, U.S. manufacturing job losses have been extreme compared to those experienced in peer countries. Of the ten countries tracked by the U.S. Bureau of Labor Statistics, no country (other than Great Britain) lost a greater share of its manufacturing jobs than the United States did between 1997 and 2009.[8] In fact, since 1997, the United States has lost 43 percent of its full-time equivalent (FTE) manufacturing workers when controlling for labor force growth, while Germany has lost just 8 percent.

Rather, the severe manufacturing job losses of the 2000s were the result of a loss of global competitiveness—in part exacerbated by other nations' unfair trade practices—which were manifested in real output declines. Official government figures suggest that U.S. manufacturing output grew by 15 percent during the 2000s, even as U.S. GDP grew by 17 percent. However, as ITIF explains in detail in *The Case for a National Manufacturing Strategy*, official government figures significantly overstate manufacturing output. A key reason why is that they overstate output from the computer and electronics sector (NAICS 334), thereby inflating estimates of overall manufacturing output growth.[9] (The government's inflated calculation of output from the computer and electronics sector pertains partly to its inability to accurately account for import substitution and partly to counting increases in computing speeds and power as increases in output). This over-estimation of the output growth from the computer and electronic products sector has masked declines across the majority of U.S. manufacturing sectors and inflated output growth from the manufacturing sector as a whole. In fact, when calculated accurately, during the 2000s, U.S. manufacturing output actually fell by 11 percent during a period when GDP increased by 17 percent.[10] This falling U.S. manufacturing output was replaced with more imported products, as America's goods trade deficit exceeded $7 trillion in the 2000s.[11]

The 2010s have seen American manufacturing rebound, yet not significantly more than one would expect from a cyclical recovery and certainly not sufficiently to suggest that structural challenges have been sufficiently addressed or that an American manufacturing renaissance is inevitable.[12] On the positive side, as the Reshoring Institute's Harry Moser notes, we've stabilized the wave of offshoring experienced during the 2000s, with the United States reshoring roughly one manufacturing job for every one offshored today.[13] (This is a significant improvement from a net loss of about 150,000 manufacturing jobs per year ten years ago.) And the United States has added 650,000 manufacturing jobs since the end of 2010.[14]

However, these job gains barely recover one-tenth of U.S. manufacturing job losses from the 2000s. Moreover, when one excludes the U.S. computer and electronics sector (again, because government data overstates this sector's output), U.S. manufacturing value added has still not recovered from the Great Recession, and in 2012 remained 7.4 percent below 2007 levels.[15] (In fact, excluding computer and electronics, from 2007 to 2012, real value added produced by durables manufacturing fell by 2.9 percent, while from 2007 to 2013 non-durables value added fell by 5.9 percent). There are still fewer U.S. factories today than there were two years ago, as 3,000 more manufacturing establishments closed then opened in 2012.[16] And our trade balance in goods is already negative $2.8 trillion for this decade.[17] In short, while U.S. manufacturing performance is better than in the 2000s, it's still not adequate. For it to be, we should be seeing manufacturing output and jobs increase at least 50 percent faster than GDP and the trade deficit in manufacturing dropping by at least 5 to 10 percent annually.

Those who believe that America's manufacturing recovery has already "turned the corner" largely believe that simply getting the "business climate" right and costs low enough are all that's needed for American manufacturing to thrive. For example, The Boston Consulting Group (BCG) recently released a report, *The U.S. as One of the Developed World's Lowest-Cost Manufacturers*, which argues that U.S. manufacturing could add at least 2.5 million and as many as 5 million new jobs by 2020, as the long-running trend of U.S. manufacturers outsourcing production to China will be reversed and replaced by a dramatic "reshoring" of manufacturing production back to the United States.[18] BCG's report contends that lower manufacturing costs will be the secret elixir restoring American manufacturing to health, citing slow increases in manufacturing wages and significantly lower energy costs.[19] Specifically, BCG holds that, by 2015, U.S. manufacturing costs will be 8 to 18 percent lower than those of leading competitors in Germany, France, Japan, and the United Kingdom and argues that "as a result of this increasing competitiveness in manufacturing, America will capture $70 to $115 billion in annual exports from other nations by the end of the decade."[20]

To be sure, U.S. manufacturing production costs have become more globally competitive. The dollar has depreciated slightly (10 percent against China's renminbi), and U.S. energy costs, such as for natural gas, have fallen to one-third European levels, attracting additional foreign direct investment and making America more competitive in energy-intensive manufacturing.[21] Yet the reality is that U.S. manufacturing costs *are already very low*, in fact below those of Germany, France, Japan, and the United Kingdom and almost on par with those of South Korea. In fact, based on an analysis of data from MAPI and the Manufacturing Institute's *2011 Report on The Structural Cost of U.S. Manufacturing*, manufacturing costs per worker hour are $29.83 in the United States, compared to $24.71 in South Korea. And manufacturing costs per worker hour are already almost 40 percent greater in Japan and almost two-thirds greater in Germany.[22] Moreover, the gap between manufacturing wages in the United States and China remains much wider than many suspect. In fact, the latest Bureau of Labor Statistics figures suggest that Chinese wages are still only approximately 20 percent of U.S. wages. And the fastest areas of foreign direct investment growth in China are in the inland areas (rather than the coastal regions) where wage levels are even lower.[23] And while lower energy costs, particularly for natural gas, will boost U.S. manufacturing competitiveness, the reality is that less than 10 percent of U.S. manufacturing output is significantly energy-intensive to the extent that lower energy costs would have a more than minor impact on total costs. For example, lower energy costs will have only a marginal impact on factories making such technology- and knowledge-intensive products as semiconductors.

Thus, while further production cost reduction will help U.S. manufacturers, they won't be sufficient to restore America's manufacturing competitiveness. So, while BCG and others who assert that an American manufacturing renaissance is right around the corner are correct that the United States can become an industrial powerhouse again, they are wrong that market forces acting alone will produce such a result. Lower costs alone won't restore the erosion of an industrial commons that has left America unable to manufacture a range of advanced high-technology products from fabless semiconductor chips to LCD screens and lithium polymer batteries.[24] Nor will lower manufacturing costs address the rampant innovation mercantilist practices of countries such as China and India that use tools such as localization barriers to trade that force American establishments to manufacture locally if they desire access to foreign markets.

Rather, it will take a coordinated set of policies regarding the "4Ts" of Technology, Trade, Tax, and Talent to power sustained American industrial renewal, as the following section elaborates.[25]

Regarding technology, America must do better at turning scientific discoveries into new technologies that are commercialized and manufactured at scale in the United States. To support this, Congress should pass the bipartisan Revitalize American Manufacturing & Innovation (RAMI) Act, which would provide one-time funding to establish up to 15 Institutes for Manufacturing Innovation. These Institutes would focus on developing advanced manufacturing product and process technologies, facilitating commercialization, and providing important workforce skills.[26] Virtually every major American manufacturing competitor—including Germany, France, Japan, and the UK—operates similar public-private partnerships focused on industrially relevant R&D and production technologies, and the United States should do so as well.[27]

The United States also needs to increase incentives for businesses to invest in R&D and innovation. The U.S. R&D tax credit is only the world's 27th most generous, behind even Brazil, China, and India.[28] Moreover, the United States lacks an investment tax credit. To remedy this, Congress should implement an Innovation and Investment Tax Credit (IITC) which would provide a tax credit of 45 percent for business investments in R&D and skills training and 25 percent on expenditures for new equipment and software on all expenditures above 50 percent of base-period expenditures.[29]

Corporate tax reform is also needed. We hear much about how while the U.S. statutory corporate rate may be second highest in the world, the U.S. effective rate is more competitive. But out of 37 nations examined, ITIF's report *The Atlantic Century* found that the United States ranks 35th highest in terms of its overall effective corporate tax rate. Moreover, of ten nations with data going back to 1989, only the United States saw an *increase* in its effective corporate tax rate.[30] Likewise, a recent National Bureau of Economic Research working paper found that of 20 nations and regions, the United States had the second highest effective corporate tax rate (with Japan the highest).[31] America's higher corporate tax rates mean that American manufacturers pay an effective tax rate 37 percent higher than Asian manufacturers do.[32] Furthermore, while broader corporate tax reform is needed, it's important that incentives for investment are not just retained but expanded as part of that process.

Finally, one in three U.S. manufacturing jobs depends on exports. Congress plays a vital role in advancing policies supporting trade promotion, trade enforcement, and opening new markets.[33] First, regarding trade promotion, the U.S. Export-Import Bank plays a vital role in supporting U.S. exports and jobs, in part by leveling the playing field for U.S. exporters by matching the credit support that other nations provide.[34] The Bank's importance has only increased as competitors such as China and Germany invest four and five times as much, respectively, than the United States as a share of their GDP in export credit.[35] It's imperative in coming weeks that Congress renew the Ex-Im Bank's authorization while increasing its lending cap.

The global trade system can produce prosperity for all, but only if nations play by the rules. Thus, while increasing exports is important, so is combatting foreign "innovation mercantilist" trade policies that seek to advantage their domestic producers at the expense of U.S. manufacturers.[36] These include, among others: currency manipulation; export subsidies; discriminatory tariffs and technology standards; intellectual property (IP) theft; localization barriers to trade (LBTs); and forced IP or technology transfer as a condition of market access. Such policies inflict significant damage on both the U.S. and global economy (and over the long term even the countries that use them), but unfortunately their use reached an all-time high in 2012, with over 1,560 technical barriers to trade reported to the World Trade Organization (WTO).[37]

In fact, just one type of innovation mercantilist tool, local content requirements (LCRs), impacts 5 percent of global trade and costs the global economy over $100 billion annually.[38] Meanwhile, innovation mercantilist practices are increasingly impacting digital industries. For example, some two dozen countries have introduced localization barriers to digital trade, including local data storage laws or requirements, such as Vietnam's Decree 72, that mandate that Internet companies must use local IT facilities in the provision of digital services.[39] India has introduced a Preferential Market Access (PMA) policy that favors Indian-based ICT manufacturers in government procurement. Brazil's public procurement policies strongly encourage domestic production by establishing price preferences of up to 25 percent across a number of sectors, including for medical technologies and medications, automobile production, and electricity generation. And China has deployed a wide range of innovation mercantilist practices, excelling at mandating technology and intellectual property transfer as a condition of market access, forcing joint ventures, introducing technology standards that favor domestic industries, showering domestic technology companies with subsidies, using anti-trust policy as a club against foreign companies, using the legal system to support use of foreign IP without due compensation, and pressuring state-owned enterprises to purchase Chinese-produced technology.

There are a number of steps Congress can take to help combat unfair foreign trade practices. First, as ITIF documents in a forthcoming report, *The Global Mercantilist Index,* Congress should require the United States Trade Representative's Office (USTR) to rank nations according to the extent of their use of mercantilist practices—and the extent to which they specifically impact high value-added, technology-intensive U.S. manufacturing industries. Congress should also provide USTR with significantly more resources for trade enforcement. In particular, Congress should authorize and appropriate $5 million to create an Office of Globalization Strategy within USTR, run by a Deputy for Globalization Strategy. The Office would be charged with *systems thinking* about the design of U.S. trade policy in the context of globalization and would have as a key assignment developing a framework for addressing state capitalism as part of a U.S. national trade strategy. Congress should also assist companies who bring trade cases before the WTO by providing companies a 25 percent tax credit for expenditures related to bringing WTO cases. Finally, for countries that continue to persist in using innovation mercantilist practices, Congress should consider precluding such countries from receiving Generalized System of Preferences (GSP) benefits.[40]

Lastly, market-access promoting free-trade agreements support U.S. exports—and jobs. Completing a comprehensive Transatlantic Trade and Investment Partnership (T-TIP) Agreement could support creation of up to 750,000 U.S. jobs over the coming decade.[41] Meanwhile, trade with Transpacific Partnership (TPP) countries supports 15 million U.S. jobs and a TPP agreement could support as many as 700,000 new U.S. jobs by 2025.[42]

While important, these agreements need to ensure very strong intellectual property protections for American intellectual property rights holders. In particular, trade secrets, or "know-how," are critical to the competitiveness of firms in innovation industries. For example, one estimate placed the value of trade secrets owned by U.S. companies at $5 trillion. Trade secrets are especially important to start-up companies and small business enterprises because, unlike patents, they can be protected without registration or formalities. But once disclosed, trade secrets lose all their value to their owners. So they must be carefully protected, especially as competitors are eager to get access to them and some foreign governments are becoming adept at forcing the disclosure of sensitive information to advance national policy goals. To address this, the T-TIP should require the adoption of a common definition for trade secrets: any information that has economic value (actual or potential), is not generally known to the public, and for which the trade secret owner has taken reasonable measures to keep private. U.S. authorities should also work with others around the world to criminalize the willful theft of trade secrets.[43]

The Information Technology Agreement (ITA)—a trade agreement which removes tariffs on trade of hundreds of information and communications technology (ICT) products—has been one of the most successful trade agreements undertaken. Since its launch in 1996, total global trade in ICT products increased more than 10 percent annually, from $1.2 trillion to over $5.0 trillion, with this growth bolstered not just by the growth of the ICT industry but also by liberalization of trade in ICT products. The ITA has empowered the formation of efficient global ICT supply chains which have enabled a shift from a closed, linear innovation model to an open innovation model that relies on close collaboration among suppliers, network partners, and customers to bring breakthrough new ICT products to market.[44] Global trade policy negotiators are currently negotiating to expand the product coverage of the ITA, as the list of ICT products the agreement covered has not been updated since the agreement's launch in 1996. ITIF estimates that expanding the Information Technology Agreement (ITA) could boost U.S. exports of information technology products by $2.8 billion annually, supporting the creation of 60,000 new jobs.[45] Congress should support the Administration's efforts to expeditiously complete these high-standard -TIP, TPP, and ITA trade agreements.

In conclusion, American manufacturing can once again become a key driver of robust economic and employment growth, but that won't happen in the absence of comprehensive public policies supporting America's manufacturing competitiveness.

Endnotes

[1] National Association of Manufacturers, "Facts About Manufacturing in the United States," http://www.nam.org/Statistics-And-Data/Facts-About-Manufacturing/Landing.aspx.

[2] Ibid.

[3] Ross DeVol et al., "Manufacturing 2.0: A More Prosperous California," The Milken Institute, June 2009, 3, http://www.milkeninstitute.org/pdf/CAManufacturing_ES.pdf; The Manufacturing Institute, *The Facts about Modern Manufacturing, 8th Edition*, 2009, http://www.nist.gov/mep/upload/FINAL_NAM_REPORT_PAGES.pdf.

[4] Stephen J. Ezell and Robert D. Atkinson, "The Case for a National Manufacturing Strategy," (Information Technology and Innovation Foundation [ITIF], 2011), http://www.itif.org/files/2011-national-manufacturing-strategy.pdf.

[5] Gregory Tassey, "Rationales and Mechanisms for Revitalizing US Manufacturing R&D Strategies," *Journal of Technology Transfer* 35, no. 3 (2010): 283-333, http://www.nist.gov/director/planning/upload/manufacturing_strategy_paper.pdf; Mark Boroush, "NSF Releases New Statistics on Business Innovation," National Science Foundation, October 2010, http://www.nsf.gov/statistics/infbrief/nsf11300/nsf11300.pdf.

[6] Robert D. Atkinson et al., "Worse Than the Great Depression: What Experts Are Missing About American Manufacturing Decline," (ITIF, March 2012), http://www2.itif.org/2012-american-manufacturing-decline.pdf.

[7] Stephen Ezell, "Revitalizing U.S. Manufacturing," *Issues in Science and Technology* Vol. 28, no. 2, (Winter 2012): 41-50, http://issues.org/28-2/ezell-3/.

[8] U.S. Bureau of Labor of Statistics, Division of International Labor Comparisons, *International Labor Comparisons of Annual Labor Fore Statistics* (Washington, D.C.: BLS, 2011), http://www.bls.gov/fls/flscomparelf/lfcompendium.pdf.

[9] Ezell and Atkinson, "The Case for a National Manufacturing Strategy," 18-21.

[10] Atkinson et al., "Worse Than the Great Depression," 3.

[11] U.S. Census Bureau, Foreign Trade (U.S. trade in goods and services—balance of payments basis; accessed December 1, 2010), http://www.census.gov/foreign-trade/statistics/historical/gands.txt.

[12] Stephen J. Ezell, "America's Manufacturing Renaissance: Fact and Fiction," (presentation, Hanover, Germany, September 17, 2013), http://www.itif.org/publications/americas-manufacturing-renaissance-fact-and-fiction.

[13] See: "Reshoring Initiative: Bringing American Jobs Back Home," http://www.reshorenow.org/.

[14] U.S. Bureau of Labor Statistics, "Employment, Hours, and Earnings from the Current Employment Statistics survey (National): Manufacturing," (accessed July 14, 2014), http://data.bls.gov/timeseries/CES3000000001.

[15] U.S. Bureau of Economic Analysis, Industry Data (GDP-by-Industry, Real Value Added by Industry, Annual; accessed July 14, 2014), http://www.bea.gov/industry/index.htm#annual.

[16] Robert D. Atkinson, "What Manufacturing Renaissance?," *The Innovation Files* (blog), April 3, 2014, http://www.innovationfiles.org/what-manufacturing-renaissance; U.S. Bureau of Labor Statistics, "2013 Business Employment Dynamics Surveys," http://www.bls.gov/schedule/archives/cewbd_nr.htm#2013.

[17] U.S. Bureau of Economic Analysis, International Data (Table 2.1, U.S. International Trade in Goods; accessed July 15, 2014), http://www.bea.gov/international/bp_web/tb_download_type_modern.cfm?list=1&RowID=45.

[18] Harold L. Sirkin, Michael Zinser, and Justin Rose, "The U.S. as One of the Developed World's Lowest-Cost Manufacturers," (The Boston Consulting Group, August 20, 2013), https://www.bcgperspectives.com/content/articles/lean_manufacturing_sourcing_procurement_behind_american_export_surge/.

[19] The Information Technology and Innovation Foundation, "ITIF Challenges the Boston Consulting Group to a Wager on the Number of American Manufacturing Jobs Added by 2020," news release, August 27, 2013, http://www.itif.org/pressrelease/itif-challenges-boston-consulting-group-wager-number-american-manufacturing-jobs-added-.

[20] Sirkin, Zisner, and Rose, ""The U.S. as One of the Developed World's Lowest-Cost Manufacturers."

[21] Robert D. Atkinson, ""The Atlantic" Story of American Manufacturing Renaissance? Think Again," *The Innovation Files* (blog), December 3, 2012, http://www.innovationfiles.org/the-atlantics-story-of-american-manufacturing-rennassaince-think-again/#sthash.1vsLQTAD.dpuf.

[22] Numbers based on analysis of data from: MAPI Manufacturers Alliance and The Manufacturing Institute, "2011 Report on The Structural Cost Of U.S. Manufacturing," (MAPI and The Manufacturing Institute, October, 2011), http://www.themanufacturinginstitute.org/Research/Structural-Cost-of-Manufacturing/2011-Structural-Cost-Report/~/media/48CE1E3848B446ADAFEBF9E945D26FC8.ashx.

[23] Economist Intelligence Unit (EIU), "China's second- and third-tier cities: Opportunities for Australia," (EIU, 2011), www.austrade.gov.au/ArticleDocuments/2045/EIU_Report_Chinas_second_and_third_tier_cities.pdf.aspx.

[24] Gary P. Pisano and Willy C. Shih, "Restoring American Competitiveness," *Harvard Business Review*, July-August 2009, http://dailyreporter.com/files/2012/11/restoring-american-competitiveness1.pdf.

[25] Stephen Ezell and Robert D. Atkinson, "Fifty Ways to Leave Your Competitiveness Woes Behind: A National Traded Sector Competitiveness Strategy," (ITIF, September 2012), http://www2.itif.org/2012-fifty-ways-competitiveness-woes-behind.pdf.

[26] Robert D. Atkinson, "Manufacturing Institutes: A Key to Revitalizing U.S. Manufacturing," *Ideas Lab*, January 30, 2014, http://www.ideaslaboratory.com/2014/01/30/manufacturing-institutes-a-key-to-revitalizing-u-s-manufacturing/.

[27] David M. Hart, Stephen J. Ezell, and Robert D. Atkinson, "A National Network for Manufacturing Innovation: Why America Needs It and How It Should Work," (ITIF, December 2012), http://www2.itif.org/2012-national-network-manufacturing-innovation.pdf.

[28] Luke A. Stewart, Jacek Warda, and Robert D. Atkinson "We're #27: The United States Lags Far Behind in R&D Tax Incentive Generosity" (ITIF, July 2012), http://www2.itif.org/2012-were-27-b-index-tax.pdf.

[29] The Information Technology and Innovation Foundation, "Top Policy Recommendations For the Obama Administration to Help the United States Win the Race for Global Advantage," (ITIF, November 2012), 2, http://www2.itif.org/2012-top-recommendations-obama-administration.pdf.

[30] *Hearing on Tax Reform Options: Incentives for Capital Investment and Manufacturing, Before the Senate Finance Committee United States Senate* (2012) (written testimony of Robert D. Atkinson, ITIF), 7, http://www2.itif.org/2012-senate-finance-manufacturing.pdf.
(2014) (written testimony of Arvind Subramanian, Center for Global Development), 6, http://www.usitc.gov/press_room/documents/testimony/332_543_001.pdf.

[31] Kevin S. Markle and Douglas A. Shackelford, "Cross-Country Comparisons of Corporate Income Taxes," *National Tax Journal* 65 (3), (September 2012): 493–528.

[32] Ibid.

[33] The White House, "Remarks by the President Announcing the President's Export Council," news release, July 7, 2010, http://www.whitehouse.gov/the-press-office/remarks-president-announcing-presidents-export-council.

[34] Robert D. Atkinson, "A Vote Against the Ex-Im Bank is a Vote Against U.S. Manufacturers," *Industry Week*, July 1, 2014, http://www.industryweek.com/public-policy/vote-against-ex-im-bank-vote-against-us-manufacturers-0.

[35] Stephen Ezell, "Foreign Export Credit Competition Continues to Intensify as U.S. Competitiveness Wanes," *The Innovation Files* (blog), July 1, 2014, http://www.innovationfiles.org/foreign-export-credit-competition-continues-to-intensify-as-u-s-competitiveness-wanes/.

[36] Stephen Ezell and Robert D. Atkinson, *The Good, The Bad, and the Ugly (and the Self-destructive) of Innovation Policy: A Policymaker's Guide to Crafting Effective Innovation Policy* (Washington, DC: ITIF, October 2010), http://www.itif.org/files/2010-good-bad-ugly.pdf.

[37] Stephen J. Ezell, Robert D. Atkinson, and Michelle A. Wein, "Localization Barriers to Trade: Threat to the Global Innovation Economy," (ITIF, September 2013), 5, http://www2.itif.org/2013-localization-barriers-to-trade.pdf.

[38] Gary Clyde Hufbauer et al., *Local Content Requirements: A Global Problem* (Washington, DC: The Peterson Institute for International Economics, September 2013), xxi.

[39] Ezell, Atkinson, and Wein, "Localization Barriers to Trade: Threat to the Global Innovation Economy."

[40] Ezell and Atkinson, "Fifty Ways to Leave Your Competitiveness Woes Behind."

[41] The Atlantic Council, Bertelsmann Foundation, and British Embassy in Washington, "TTIP and the Fifty States: Jobs and Growth from Coast to Coast," (The Atlantic Council, 2013), 3, http://www.atlanticcouncil.org/images/publications/TTIP_and_the_50_States_WEB.pdf.

[42] The U.S. Chamber of Commerce, "TPP Could Create 700,000 New U.S. Jobs,"

[43] Michelle A. Wein and Stephen J. Ezell, "How to Craft an Innovation Maximizing T-TIP Agreement," (ITIF, October 2013), http://www.itif.org/publications/how-craft-innovation-maximizing-t-tip-agreement.

[44] Osamu Onodera, "Trade and Innovation Project: A Synthesis Paper" (working paper, OECD, Paris, August 7, 2008), 4, http://www.oecd.org/dataoecd/60/22/41105505.pdf.

[45] Stephen J. Ezell, "Boosting Exports, Jobs, and Economic Growth by Expanding the ITA," (ITIF, March 2012), http://www2.itif.org/2012-boosting-exports-jobs-expanding-ita.pdf.

STATEMENT OF HON. ORRIN G. HATCH, RANKING MEMBER
U.S. SENATE COMMITTEE ON FINANCE HEARING OF JULY 17, 2014
THE ROLE OF TRADE AND TECHNOLOGY IN 21st CENTURY MANUFACTURING

WASHINGTON – U.S. Senator Orrin Hatch (R-Utah), Ranking Member of the Senate Finance Committee, today issued the following statement regarding the Finance Committee hearing on the role of trade and technology in the 21st century manufacturing:

Thank you, Mr. Chairman, for holding this hearing on the role of trade and technology in 21st century manufacturing.

The success of our manufacturing sector is vital.

Nearly 12 million Americans are directly employed in manufacturing – that's nearly one out of ten American jobs. This is true in my state, where nearly 10 percent of working Utahns are employed in manufacturing.

That's 120,000 jobs in Utah alone.

That's one reason I'm happy Ray Kimber is here with us today.

I often talk about the small, innovative company that begins in a garage and grows to become a driver of economic growth and a source of jobs.

That's Kimber Kable.

Twenty five years ago, Mr. Kimber figured out a way to weave audio cables to reduce unwanted noise and improve fidelity. He founded Kimber Kable to manufacture those cables, and now he employs 30 people in Ogden, Utah.

He sells his cables to the world.

Today, two-thirds of Kimber cables are shipped to customers overseas.

Ray is not only a friend, he is also an outstanding example of a larger truth that the U.S. manufacturing sector is the most innovative in the world, and American workers are unsurpassed in manufacturing productivity.

Because of U.S. innovation and productivity, in those areas where U.S. manufacturing competes on an equal footing, it succeeds.

Our manufacturers maintain a trade surplus of $60 billion per year with the 20 countries where we have a free trade agreement in place. And, per capita, the consumers from those countries purchase nearly 13 times more U.S. goods than consumers from the rest of the world.

Where you find a market that is open and secured by strong international trade rules, you will find goods, like Mr. Kimber's, that are manufactured in America.

Put simply, U.S. trade agreements are good for U.S. manufacturers.

But we need to do a better job opening overseas markets and making sure our manufacturers don't face discrimination and other trade barriers.

There are several negotiations underway with our partners in the Pacific region, in Europe, and at the World Trade Organization that will help address the challenges faced by U.S. manufacturers.

But I don't think any of these efforts are going to succeed without Trade Promotion Authority, or TPA.

Without TPA, the administration is severely handicapped in negotiating high-quality agreements that will benefit American manufacturers and achieve the goals of Congress.

That is why, in January, former Senator Baucus and I introduced the Bipartisan Congressional Trade Priorities Act, which would renew TPA, and empower our trade negotiators to bring home trade agreements that meet the high standards set by Congress and to see those agreements passed into law.

Importantly, the bill sets negotiating objectives for our agreements. I want to highlight two of those today.

We have witnesses with us here today representing companies that have created and taken advantage of advances in technology. Part of getting their products around the world is digital trade. That is why the TPA bill we introduced requires U.S. trade agreements to ensure that electronically delivered goods and services are classified with the most liberal trade treatment possible, and that our trading partners allow the free flow of data across borders.

But using the Internet to market, sell, and transmit digital products is only part of the story.

These companies are also innovators, and their innovations must be protected.

Our witnesses today have experienced firsthand the destructive impact of intellectual property theft. Mr. Kimber, for example, has had to contend with counterfeiters stealing his company's name to sell inferior products.

Our TPA bill also requires that U.S. trade agreements reflect a standard of intellectual property rights protection similar to that found in U.S. law. And, it calls for an end to the theft of U.S. intellectual property by foreign governments, including piracy and the theft of trade secrets, and for the elimination of measures that require U.S. companies to locate their intellectual property abroad in return for market access.

For our manufacturers to continue to succeed overseas, we must also ensure our companies are able to exploit global supply chains so they can access the best inputs, add the most value to products, and ship their goods around the world as efficiently as possible.

That's why, last year, former Senator Baucus and I introduced the Trade Facilitation and Trade Enforcement Reauthorization Act to make trade facilitation a top priority at U.S. Customs and Border Protection, and to improve intellectual property rights enforcement at the border.

Trade is good for U.S. manufacturing.

Like I said, where our manufacturers operate in markets secured by free trade agreements, they succeed.

But the challenges they face around the world are only growing, and we in Congress need to do our part to help achieve the conditions overseas under which American manufacturers can thrive.

That being the case, I hope the Committee will soon be able to consider some of these pending trade bills.

We really cannot afford to wait.

Thank you, once again, Mr. Chairman. I look forward to hearing from our witnesses.

###

Testimony of Ray Kimber
Founder, Owner and President
RKB Industrial and Kimber Kable

Before the Senate Committee on Finance
United States Senate, Washington, DC
July 17, 2014

Chairman Wyden, Ranking Member Hatch, and distinguished Members of the Committee, my name is Ray Kimber. I am Founder and CEO of Kimber Kable. It is my pleasure to appear before you today on behalf of Kimber Kable and the Consumer Electronics Association. CEA owns and produces the International CES – The Global Stage for Innovation – and CEA's over-2000 member companies represent the $208 billion U.S. consumer electronics industry. Both Kimber Kable, and CEA, rely upon an open global marketplace and policies that promote free trade, and protect our innovations at home and abroad.

I founded my company in 1979 with the Kimber Kable product line. Over time, our innovations have revolutionized the field of sound technology, and we have carved a niche as global experts in sound technology and audio cable. Our product eliminates noise and improves the fidelity of entire audio/video systems.

Today, Kimber Kable employs more than 29 people in Ogden, Utah where our product is manufactured. Approximately 60–70% of the product we manufacture in Utah is exported to nearly 60 countries.

Kimber Cable is typical of U.S. manufacturers who rely on access to international markets for continued growth and success. Passage of vital trade agreements, and legislation which protects our companies' trade secrets and products, are strong examples of areas where the government can help American innovators.

I commend you, Mr. Chairman and Ranking Member, for working with industry to secure agreements and policies that U.S. companies need to be competitive.

Free Trade Agreements (FTAs) have worked for us in the past. The most recent examples – with Korea, Colombia and Panama – were designed to eliminate tariffs and non-tariff barriers, such as non-transparent regulatory processes, which are technical barriers to trade. FTAs increase confidence and certainty for U.S. industry doing business in those partner countries. In 2012, America's free trade agreement partners purchased 12.8 times more goods per capita from the United States than did other countries.[1]

We want new FTAs negotiated, and passed by congress, to establish rules-based environments where U.S. companies can operate with confidence that they have certain protections, and mechanisms for enforcement, provided by those agreements. Agreements currently under negotiation such as the Trans-Atlantic Trade and Investment Partnership and the Trade in Services Agreement can do just that, especially if they do not include harmful intermediary liability language or excessive copyright restrictions.

For those agreements to be concluded swiftly, we need FTA partners to trust that the United States has the ability to actually pass those agreements into law. Trade Promotion Authority expired in 2007, and without its renewal, we risk that negotiated trade agreements will never pass into law. That costs me, my workers in Utah, and the entire U.S. economy – and, diminishes U.S. companies' ability to innovate and remain competitive in the global marketplace.

One of the biggest challenges we at Kimber Kable face is the threat of counterfeit products. We consider the research, design and engineering of our product to be the epitome of our company's trade secrets. The numbers below represent our export percentages. You can see that we struggle to grow and retain our overseas markets.

2012 – 76.53%

2013 – 67.07%

2014 – 62.47% (year to date as of 6/30/2014)

A measureable part of the sales decline is tied to an increase in counterfeiting of our products.

In countries around the globe – from Taiwan, China, Canada and even right here in the U.S., counterfeit goods are negatively impacting our sales and our reputation. We have invested considerable time and resources to educate customers and combat the source of counterfeit products. Frustratingly, our efforts have yielded little results. Sometimes it even seems that counterfeit producers are aided – or at least protected – by local governments.

These challenges are the reason I, and all of us at Kimber Kable, are so appreciative of Senator Hatch's efforts to introduce the Customs Reauthorization Bill.

This bill would help small exporters like Kimber Kable by giving us an IP center that enables law enforcement agencies to coordinate – giving us greater effectiveness at home and abroad. The bill also authorizes and directs Customs and Border Protection to share information with IPR rights holders to help quickly determine whether a suspect product crossing the U.S. boarder violates a copyright or trademark. This is an action CEA members have long urged, as currently CBP's internal policies impede the sharing of this information. The result is that counterfeit product enters markets to the detriment of rights holders, often putting the public's safety at risk.

Part of Kimber Kable's international appeal is our commitment to remain "Made in America." To go into a new market with a "substance over sizzle" approach, requires investment. The reality is that our U.S. brand offers lower margins – and that exacerbates challenges. We must actually go to a country and educate distributors and the sub-dealer networks on the value of our product. I have little confidence that this education can reach all consumers without local governments cracking down on counterfeit producers and sellers. Enforceable free trade agreements, and legislation such as the proposed Customs Reauthorization Bill which will streamline information sharing, are very valuable actions congress can take to help domestic manufacturers like me remain globally competitive.

Finally, I want to address a pending agreement, the success of which would be a boon to our industry. The Information Technology Agreement (ITA) was negotiated over 15 years ago and has not been updated since. Products such as video games and consoles and the audio and video systems that support them are not a part of the original agreement. Updating the ITA to include these products will benefit consumers by making them more affordable and promote greater production of these devices, thereby creating jobs.

CEA and its members have been working tirelessly with USTR to advance the deal, and we could use congress' help to encourage China to return to the negotiation table prepared to make significant and meaningful progress. China's importance to us can be exemplified by one CEA member's recent sale there:

Small member company Mitek manufactures speakers in Ennis, TX where they employ about 150 people. They manufacture finished product Louisville, KY where they employ about 100 partners, and manufacture electronic components for products in Phoenix where they employ about 100 partners.

Mitek recently outfitted the Shanghai Airport and the Shenzhen ferry station with U.S. made paging systems.

Amazingly, speakers systems carry a whopping 40 % tariff rate into China! With that 40% duty removed, imagine our selling potential to those millions of customers.

This agreement is of particular importance to Kimber Kable because more speaker, amplifier, gaming and video product sales around the world, means more cable sales for us.

We believe a deal is within reach this year, but for that to happen, we need continued high level political engagement from the U.S. government.

If the U.S. is not pursuing new agreements, we risk falling behind other countries that are passing agreements at a rapid pace. To help domestic manufacturers like Kimber Kable, our government must continue to pursue new legislation such as the Customs Reauthorization Act that helps battle counterfeit product, and Trade Promotion Authority so trade deals will pass through congress quickly. Successfully concluding T-TIP, and the Trade in Services Agreement, and Congress' help pressuring China to return to the table on ITA, are areas where congress can help immediately.

Thank you again for the opportunity to testify, and I will be pleased to respond to any questions the Committee may have.

---

[1] Business Roundtable (2013). "How the U.S. Economy Benefits from International Trade and Investment." Derived from The Trade Partnership.
(http://www.tradepartnership.com/site/data.html) and World Bank population estimates.

PREPARED STATEMENT FOR THE RECORD OF INTEL CORPORATION

For the

UNITED STATES SENATE COMMITTEE ON FINANCE

On

THE ROLE OF TRADE AND TECHNOLOGY IN 21ST CENTURY MANUFACTURING

July 17, 2014

Intel Corporation respectfully submits this statement for the record in conjunction with the Senate Finance Committee's hearing on The Role of Trade and Technology in 21st Century Manufacturing. Our statement will focus on the importance of increasing market access overseas as a way to create and maintain U.S. manufacturing jobs. This objective is critical to the continued growth and leadership of the United States, and must be a top priority as U.S. industries face escalating competition overseas and an increasing number of governments strike preferential trade deals with other significant economies. Open and robust trade has proven time and again to improve economic welfare globally.

The U.S. government can increase market access for U.S. companies in three important ways: (i) expand existing free trade agreements (FTAs) so they cover more markets and additional goods and services; (ii) negotiate additional robust FTAs on an accelerated basis; and (iii) use a combination of mechanisms (e.g., modernized agreements and promotion of best practices) to address emerging non-tariff barriers not covered by existing trade rules. These three recommendations are dealt with in detail in Sections III, IV and V below. Before delving into those recommendations, however, we first provide some background information in Sections I and II that should help the Committee better understand our industry and why it is so important to ensure the U.S. government's trade agenda promotes 21st century manufacturing.

I.   **Market Access is Critical for our Industry**

1.   Intel Depends on Overseas Markets to Create and Sustain Jobs at Home

In 1968, Robert Noyce and Gordon Moore, two scientists who helped build Fairchild Semiconductor, decided to leave that company and form their own business to manufacture semiconductor memory products. Soon after, a third visionary named Andy Grove, a Hungarian immigrant, joined the team. The new company, Intel Corporation, began with 12 employees, limited cash, and $2.5 million in venture capital.

Today, Intel is the world's largest semiconductor manufacturer by revenue, and powering everything from phones and tablets to supercomputers and servers. We have over 100,000 employees worldwide, with more than half of them based in the U.S. Our revenue last year was about $53 billion, generated from sales to customers in more than 120 countries.

Our company is a prime example of why the U.S. government should increase U.S. exports by opening up new markets and removing or reducing existing trade barriers overseas. More than three quarters of our revenue comes from sales outside the U.S., while roughly three quarters of our advanced microprocessor manufacturing and R&D is done here across 23 states with major operations in Arizona, California, New Mexico and Oregon. The revenue we generate outside the U.S. helps create and sustain our investments and high paying jobs here at home.

Semiconductor manufacturing is extremely expensive, requiring significant capital investment, R&D, exotic materials science, extremely sophisticated tools, complex construction technology for mega factories, and a vast variety of services to keep those factories running smoothly. Our global R&D investment in 2013 alone was $10.6 billion and our capital investments that same year were $10.7 billion. In 2012, Intel was the No.1 investor in R&D among U.S. publicly traded companies and the 5th largest capital investor in the U.S.

A leading edge factory now costs about $5 billion when fully equipped and costs much more to run the factory over its operating life. With a new technology generation developed every two years, many new very expensive tools are purchased to implement the technology and make ever smaller transistors. This dynamic technology treadmill means that our suppliers are critical to Intel's success.

In other words, access to foreign markets does not impact just Intel and its employees. We have over 16,000 suppliers worldwide. More than 7,300 of our suppliers are U.S. based, located in 46 states, with over 3,000 of those suppliers being classified as small businesses. Intel spent almost $3 billion in 2013 on goods and services purchased just from U.S. small businesses in industry sectors that vary from the supply of chemical gases to the supply of construction services. Those purchases are fueled by overseas demand for our products. Overseas demand, in turn, allows us to "export" our high labor and environmental standards as we share them with our foreign suppliers and implement them in our operations in other countries.

We are proud to be an economic engine in the communities where we do our cutting-edge manufacturing. In addition, to the direct economic impacts of our manufacturing and R&D investments, Intel also has a substantial multiplier effect on job growth and U.S. GDP. For every Intel job in the U.S., an additional 13 American jobs are supported, resulting in a total of 774,600 jobs. Intel's direct impact on U.S. GDP in 2012 was $26 billion. When the multiplier effect through Intel's supply chain and distribution channels is taken into account, the impact on U.S. GDP in 2012 alone was more than $96 billion.[1]

We have spent more than $68 billion on U.S. operations, manufacturing and R&D, from 2002 to 2011. Most of the product manufactured from our U.S. investments will be sold to the 95% of consumers that live overseas. Access to global markets is essential to Intel's continued growth and our ability to create and maintain jobs in the U.S.

2. The Entire Semiconductor Industry's Future is Tied to Overseas Sales

According to the Semiconductor Industry Association (SIA), the U.S. semiconductor industry directly employs about 250,000 employees, supports approximately 1 million indirect jobs in the U.S. and makes almost half of the world's computer chips. This market for chips was worth about $306 billion in 2013 and is growing every year.[2] In fact, between 1987 and 2011 (the year with most recent data), the semiconductor industry grew 265% and contributed the most to U.S. GDP among all U.S. major manufacturing industries.[3]

Free trade is of particular importance to the growth of the entire semiconductor industry. Over 80% of U.S. semiconductors go to customers outside the U.S. market and are sold in nearly every country in the world. According to the International Trade Commission

---

[1] "Intel's Economic Impacts on the U.S. Economy, 2008-2012," PWC (December 17, 2013); available at: http://www.intel.com/content/www/us/en/company-overview/us-economic-impact-study.html.

[2] World Semiconductor Trade Statistics (2013).

[3] Contribution to GDP means industry's total output less intermediary products and services. Sources cited: Bureau of Economic Analysis: Benchmark Input-Output Tables 1987-2007 and U.S. Bureau of Census: Annual Survey of Manufactures 2011 (refreshed and converted to 2009 dollars with BEA's real and current GDP tables).

(ITC), the semiconductor industry is among America's largest exporters; in 2013, semiconductors were America's number one electronic product exports and they were a top three manufactured export.[4] Yet, as discussed below, the information technology industry is facing an increasing number of market access issues that need to be effectively and promptly addressed.

Exporting semiconductors creates real benefits for many American workers. For example, the overseas sales allow leading-edge U.S. based chip makers to employ highly skilled and talented U.S. workers whose average income is almost $120,000 per year.[5] In 2013 alone, domestic semiconductor makers invested about $34 billion in research and development and invested over $21 billion in capital equipment. These rates of investment in R&D and capital equipment are among the highest of any U.S. industry, when measured as a share of total sales.[6] Such high investment and R&D rates spur new products and create new jobs both among our U.S. suppliers and at the semiconductor companies, which are maintained by overseas sales.

II.   Ensure U.S. Trade Policy Protects and Promotes Advanced Manufacturing

Last year, manufacturing contributed $2.08 trillion or 12.5 percent of GDP to the U.S. economy. For every $1.00 spent in manufacturing, another $1.32 is added to the U.S. economy-- the highest multiplier effect of any economic sector.[7] The average American worker in manufacturing earns about $77,500 per year or $15,000 more annually than the average worker in all U.S. industries.[8] And the average wage in *advanced* manufacturing is much higher than $77,500; for example, as noted earlier, in the semiconductor industry that wage is $120,000. Manufacturers in the U.S. perform two-thirds of all private sector R&D, driving more innovation than any other sector.[9]

As the National Association of Manufacturers makes clear in its advocacy efforts, access to foreign markets is key for manufacturers big and small in just about every industry sector. More than 97 percent of U.S. companies that export are small and medium-sized businesses with less than 500 employees.[10] U.S. employment in trade-related jobs grew six and a half times faster than total employment between 2004 and 2011.[11] And jobs linked to exports pay, on average, 18 percent more than other jobs.[12]

---

[4] U.S. International Trade Commission, Dataweb.

[5] U.S. Bureau of Labor Statistics (BLS). *See also*:
http://www.semiconductors.org/clientuploads/Jobs%20Rollout/Jobs%20Issue%20Paper_April_2013.pdf.

[6] IC Insights, Inc. – The McClean Report 2014 and WSTS.

[7] Bureau of Economic Analysis, Industry Economic Accounts (2012).

[8] *Id.*

[9] National Science Foundation (2008). For more statistics about manufacturing in the U.S., please visit the National Association of Manufacturers web site at http://www.nam.org/Statistics-And-Data/Facts-About-Manufacturing/Landing.aspx.

[10] U.S. Department of Commerce, U.S. Exporters in 2011: A Statistical Overview; available at http://www.trade.gov/mas/ian/smeoutlook/tg_ian_001925.asp.

[11] Baughman and Francois, Trade and American Jobs, The Impact of Trade on U.S. and State Level Employment: An Update (2010); available at http://businessroundtable.org/uploads/studies-reports/downloads/Trade_and_American_Jobs.pdf; Business Roundtable, How the U.S. Economy Benefits from International Trade and Investment; available at http://businessroundtable.org/sites/default/files/legacy/uploads/general/BRT_State_Studies_-_US_Total.pdf.

[12] Riker, Do Jobs in Exports Still Pay More? And Why?, U.S. Department of Commerce

With 95% of the world's consumers living outside of the U.S. and about 80% of global purchasing power outside the U.S., any increase in domestic manufacturing must be accompanied by additional opportunities to sell overseas. In the aggregate, U.S. manufacturing industries can do much better in selling overseas into an $11 trillion global market for manufactured goods.[13] The World Economic Forum Global Competitiveness Report for 2012-2013 listed the United States near the bottom, or 138th out of 144 economies, for exports of goods as a percentage of gross domestic product. And, even though U.S. exports in manufactured goods have grown steadily in recent years, we have lost market share to even more rapidly growing exports of goods from key emerging markets.[14]

Opportunities to sell manufactured goods overseas are created in large part by the negotiation and enforcement of new free trade agreements (FTAs), bilateral investment treaties (BITs), and other initiatives that establish the rules to force open additional markets and promote and protect U.S. business interests. The Committee can help ensure that trade rules take into account 21st century manufacturing. Every major government wants more domestic manufacturing to create additional jobs and boost their economy--especially advanced manufacturing with its high paying jobs. These governments are under pressure to take shortcuts by using trade distortive measures to build up local manufacturing.

In brief, there are still many old barriers that must be taken down and emerging barriers that need to be removed before they are implemented. For example, a study conducted last year that reviewed more than 100 policies imposing local content requirements (LCRs) in numerous countries and industries found that LCRs reduce global trade activities by as much as $93 billion annually.[15] LCRs are becoming especially pernicious and pervasive in the high tech sector because it is considered a strategic industry and thus targeted for local development by many foreign governments. LCRs in our sector also involved forced technology transfer as a condition for investment or to gain market access. As noted recently by USTR, these measures can take the form of standards and regulatory approvals that are discriminatory, incentives based on the origin of IP, and governments allowing national firms to infringe IP owned by foreign firms.[16]

There is no panacea for leveling the playing field for U.S. manufacturers. As noted below, the U.S. government must use a variety of mechanisms to further increase our exports, improve our economy and thus create more U.S. jobs. Existing FTAs need to be expanded where possible so they cover more markets and additional goods and services. The U.S. government also needs to enter into additional FTAs on an accelerated basis without sacrificing their quality. Also, industries with trade supportive governments must work ever more closely together to shun and isolate protectionism, and show that open markets work best in the global economy. And, at some point, Congress may want to address how to make Trade Adjustment Assistance more effective for those workers who are displaced by trade flows.

Manufacturing and Services Brief (July 2010), accessed at
http://trade.gov/mas/ian/build/groups/public/@tg_ian/documents/webcontent/tg_ian_003208.pdf.
[13] Source: National Association of Manufacturers.
[14] "In terms of global market share of manufactured exports, the U.S. share declined from 18 percent in 2000 to 9 percent in 2012." Manufacturers Alliance for Productivity and Innovation (citing World Bank and Eurostat); available at through 2012): http://www.manufacturingfacts.org/single-project_32.html.
[15] Gary Clyde Hufbauer and Jeffrey J. Schott, *Local Content Requirements: A Global Problem,* Peterson Institute for International Economics (September 2013).
[16] USTR Special 301 Report (2014), pp. 17-18.

III. **Increase U.S. Exports by Expanding the Scope of Existing Agreements**

Too many key markets are still subject to too few existing trade rules. We discuss several examples in this section involving multilateral agreements.

1. Continue Pushing to Expand the Product Coverage and Membership of the ITA

Intel strongly supports the Obama Administration's extensive efforts over the last several years to expand the product coverage of the Information Technology Agreement (ITA). We also appreciate the Administration's efforts to expand ITA's original membership by making ITA accession a requirement for membership in the Trans-Pacific Partnership (TPP) Agreement. We hope both these negotiations can be concluded quickly.

The intent of the WTO Information Technology Agreement (ITA), negotiated some 18 years ago with strong bipartisan support,[17] was to promote the development of the emerging global digital economy at the lowest possible cost.[18] By eliminating customs tariffs on a range of information communication technology (ICT) products in many countries, the ITA has dramatically increased U.S. exports. In fact, as noted earlier, semiconductors have been one of the largest U.S. exports over the last five years.

From 1996, when the ITA was signed, to 2008, total trade in ITA listed goods has increased more than 10 percent annually, from $1.2 trillion to $4.0 trillion. The dissemination of ICT without customs tariffs in many parts of the world has enabled more ICT use that, in turn, has had a significant positive impact on the global economy by increasing productivity; creating high paying jobs and more efficient markets; raising the quality of innovation, goods, services and innovation; improving health care and education; and otherwise enhancing the quality of life.

But Mexico, Brazil and several other notable countries are not ITA signatories. And, more importantly, many of the digital products developed in the last eighteen years -- such as multi-component semiconductors, video game consoles, e-readers, and DRAMs, video game consoles, and flat panel displays -- are not covered by the ITA.

ITA expansion of its product coverage would increase U.S. exports of ICT products by $2.8 billion, boost revenues of U.S. ICT firms by $10 billion, and support creation of approximately 60,000 new U.S. jobs.[19] Preliminary industry studies indicate that an expanded ITA could remove tariffs on an additional $1 trillion in global ICT trade, with more than $122 billion in U.S. ICT trade affected.

Semiconductors constitute the largest product category covered by the ITA in terms of value. From 2005 to 2010, semiconductor products experienced the highest export growth rate

---

[17] The agreement is formally known as the "Ministerial Declaration on Trade in Information Technology Products," and was signed in Singapore on December 13, 1996 (WTO ref. WT/MIN(96)/16).

[18] As former USTR Charlene Barshefsky put it, "The Information Technology Agreement . . . means that the creation of the information superhighway will be encouraged and promoted, not taxed." Statement at the conclusion of the Singapore Ministerial of the WTO (December 1996).

[19] This estimate assumes an average tariff of non-ITA covered ICT products of 5.3% and an average trade-weighted import demand elasticity of ITA members of 1.30. (ITIF Report, March 2012).

of any ITA product category, growing at 7.8 percent annually. By 2010, semiconductors accounted for 33 percent of global exports of ICT products[20] and have since remained one of our country's top exports.

As an example of the value of expanding the ITA, consider multi chip components (MCOs). This developing semiconductor product, which contains multiple types of individual components as opposed to a single integrated circuit, accounts for roughly 1.5 to3 percent of the global semiconductor market today. However, we anticipate this percentage to significantly increase going forward. If ITA expansion includes MCOs, it has been estimated that its manufacturers would enjoy nearly $200 million in tariff savings per year.[21]

2.   Expand Membership of the GPA

Government procurement comprises a significant share of the global economy -- from 10-to-20 percent of the GDP for many countries. And, while estimates vary widely, many believe that global government procurement is a multi-trillion dollar market with the contestable share (i.e., the amount subject to international competition) being around 30% of that value.[22]

Yet, none of the BRIC countries are signatories to the WTO Government Procurement Agreement (GPA) that prevents discrimination against foreign suppliers. This has enabled the BRICs to promulgate measures designed to favor local suppliers, especially those in the electronics sector, as a way to unfairly build up and favor local companies and ICT related industries. Unfortunately, such policies not only will hurt U.S. companies, but also raise consumer prices and limit product choice within the countries promulgating them.

Brazil's government purchases domestically produced goods and services, even when these cost up to 25% more than the cheapest imported products and services, if they are developed by Brazilian companies that (i) manufacture the goods at issue in Brazil or provide the services locally; and (ii) invest a certain percentage of revenue in R&D and the development of technology in the country. Implementing regulations, which typically require an increasing amount of local content each year to qualify for the preferences, are focused on defense, healthcare and ICT.[23]

The Ministry of Communications and Information Technology (MCIT) of India, for its part, recommended in 2011 that government procurement preferences be given to all domestically produced electronic products and products made with Indian IP. [24] Moreover, MCIT attempted to extend domestic government procurement preferences in the telecom sector to cover private licensees, even though that would violate the national treatment clause of the

---

[20] "ITA Report," The Information Technology and Innovation Foundation (April 2014) ["ITIF Report"].

[21] ITIF Report, April 2014.

[22] The Size of Government Procurement Markets, OECD (2002) (using 1998 data), accessed at http://www.oecd.org/dataoecd/34/14/1845927.pdf; International Trade Statistics, World Trade Organization (2009) (using 2008 goods data), accessed at http://www.wto.org/english/res_e/statis_e/its2009_e/its2009_e.pdf; Options for Global Trade Reform: A View from the Asia-Pacific (Trade and Development), edited by Will Martin and Mari Pangestu (2003) at 249.

[23] Government Purchase Law (No. 8.666, promulgated in 1993).

[24] Progress Report on the 100-Days Plan of Action of Ministry of Communications & Information Technology Announced on January 01 This Year (April 11, 2011), DoT Action Point 8(c) and DIT Action Point 8(c).

General Agreement on Tariffs and Trade.[25] Both the National Telecom Policy and Manufacturing Policy advance procurement preferences for domestic product in the telecom and other strategic technological sectors.[26] Several years ago, consistent with MCIT's recommendation, the Cabinet of India approved a broader proposal to provide government procurement preferences, on a graded value-add basis, to all domestically manufactured electronic products (whether for the telecom sector or not).[27] The Government of India is now implementing its procurement guideline.

In 2011, former PRC President Hu Jintao voluntarily committed his administration to breaking the links between China's indigenous innovation and government procurement policies. Subsequent commitments followed, and as a result, various central and provincial authorities took steps to toward implementing these commitments. Not all relevant authorities have taken such steps, however. Moreover, in 2012, according to a survey of the US/China Business Council (USCBC) member companies, the paper changes that had been made had not yet effectively translated into tangible sales opportunities.[28] GPA accession would make such commitments binding and enforceable.

Russia has a narrower public procurement preference program than the other BRIC countries. In 2010, the Ministry of Industry and Trade issued a decree that enables domestic manufacturers to receive preferences in state procurements tenders of telecommunication equipment for LTE networks where not less than 50% of the stock of the company belongs to the Russian state or its citizens, and the entire product cycle (e.g., R&D, manufacturing and assembly) of components (e.g., printed circuit boards) needed for the telecom equipment that the domestic company engages occurs in Russia. In addition, the qualifying manufacturer must own the rights to software used in the equipment and the required local content level for components in the telecom equipment rises each year.[29]

These types of market preferences can significantly distort trade because government procurement comprises a major share of the global economy. We need to incentivize other large governments to join the GPA with contract thresholds and coverage of regulatory authorities which are similar in scope to that provided by the U.S. More efficient, accountable, competitive and transparent procurement structures are increasingly critical for all governments, as they seek to provide their citizens with the highest quality goods and services within significant fiscal constraints.

---

[25] Pressure from the U.S. and Japanese governments influenced the Government of India to cut back its measure to government procurement.

[26] National Telecom Policy (2012), Section III(33) and IV(2.16); Manufacturing Policy (2011), Sections 1.21(i), 1.22 and 8.2.

[27] *See* http://pib.nic.in/newsite/PrintRelease.aspx?relid=80074.

[28] Status Report: China's Innovation and Government Procurement Policies," The US-China Business Council (May 2014); available at: http://www.uschina.org/reports/indigenous-innovation-and-procurement-progress-report-2014.

[29] "Order on approval of the parameter values, methods of the parameter value determination and the order of assignment of the status of the *Russian domestic telecommunications equipment* to telecommunications equipment manufactured within the territory of the Russian Federation," Ministry of Industry and Trade of the Russian Federation (July, 26th, 2010).

IV. Increase the Number of Robust FTAs on an Accelerated Basis

When trade rules are used to open markets, U.S. manufacturers can compete on a global playing field, boost sales and grow their share of foreign markets. America's 20 existing free trade agreement (FTA) partners account for less than 10 percent of the global economy but purchase nearly 50% percent of all U.S. manufactured goods exports. The United States enjoys a nearly $60 billion manufacturing trade surplus with its trade agreement partners, compared with a $508 billion deficit with other countries.

The United States, however, has not kept pace with other countries in opening new markets abroad, especially in the fast-growing economies of Asia and Latin America that are now major engines of global growth. According to WTO data, about 585 regional trade agreements (RTAs) have been negotiated worldwide and, of those, 385 RTAs have entered into force.[30] The United States is party to only 14 such agreements.[31] In contrast, the European Union has 37 RTAs, and is in negotiations with India, Canada and Japan.[32] Singapore has 21 RTAs in force and agreements pending with Canada, the EU and Ukraine.[33] And India has 16 RTAs in force and another four in negotiation.[34] Similarly, when it comes to bilateral investment treaties, the U.S. lags behind in a world with nearly 3,000 BITs. In particular, the 48 U.S. BITs in force are far less than half of Germany's 147 BITs and considerably less than China's 90 BITs or even Korea's 68 BITs.[35]

Of course, the U.S. government must be selective in allocating its limited resources and determine which governments it can negotiate with to produce the most mutual benefit. We also recognize that USTR is currently negotiating two significant agreements, which hopefully will set a high bar for subsequent FTAs.

1. Ensure a High Quality TPP Agreement that Will Serve as a Template for Other FTAs

We appreciate USTR's relentless use of resources to negotiate a robust Trans-Pacific Partnership (TPP) Agreement among 11 other countries in the Asia-Pacific region. USTR staff has exercised considerable effort to make the TPP agreement the gold standard for trade rules. Of particular interest to Intel, USTR has worked hard for language in the agreement that increases trade secret protection, enhances e-commerce provisions, prevents unnecessary regulation of commercial encryption, and provides more robust due process protections in competition cases. However, raising the bar significantly may require more time and Intel is

---

[30] "Some Figures on Regional Trade Agreements." *WTO*. 01 July 2014.
http://rtais.wto.org/UI/publicsummarytable.aspx
[31] "United States of America Country Profile." *WTO*. 01 Jul 2014.
http://rtais.wto.org/UI/PublicearchByMemberResult.aspx?MemberCode=840&lang=1&redirect=1
[32] "European Union Country Profile." *WTO*. 01 Jul 2014.
http://rtais.wto.org/UI/PublicSearchByMemberResult.aspx?MemberCode=918&lang=1&redirect=1
[33] "Singapore Country Profile." *WTO*. 01 Jul 2014.
http://rtais.wto.org/UI/PublicSearchByMemberResult.aspx?MemberCode=702&lang=1&redirect=1
[34] "India Country Profile." *WTO*. 01 Jul 2014.
http://rtais.wto.org/UI/PublicSearchByMemberResult.aspx?MemberCode=356&lang=1&redirect=1
[35] "Database of Bilateral Investment Treaties." *ICSID*. 2014.
https://icsid.worldbank.org/ICSID/FrontServlet?requestType=ICSIDPublicationsRH&actionVal=ViewBilateral&req
From=Main

concerned that the quality of the TPP agreement may be partially sacrificed as a result of the agency's strong desire to finalize negotiations this year. New provisions, such as a right to cross-border data flows subject to limited and justified exceptions, are critical to so many industries – including ours, which relies on a global supply chain. Yet such provisions take time to negotiate because, for some governments with less advanced economies the benefits are not intuitive. We would thus recommend that USTR continue to work diligently to maximize the momentum it has developed in the TPP negotiations, but not pursue an arbitrary deadline as the end goal.

2. <u>Negotiate a Comprehensive Transatlantic Trade and Investment Partnership (TTIP)</u>

Although the sixth round of negotiations on TTIP just began, so far U.S. and EC negotiators have tabled only preliminary offers (if anything at all) on the various subject matter areas under negotiation. We are nevertheless concerned that undue focus on regulatory and other differences between the U.S. and EC legal systems could negatively impact the broad, strategic scope of the TIPP agreement initially contemplated by the parties. Specifically, President Obama, European Council President Van Rompuy, and European Commission President Barroso jointly emphasized that the agreement will "not only expand trade and investment across the Atlantic, *but also contribute to the development of global rules that can strengthen the multilateral trading system.* " [36]

The greatest value of a transatlantic agreement to Intel will be the precedent it can set across the globe on sensitive policy issues. Other governments are more likely to follow when the EU and the U.S. speak with one voice on emerging trade, investment and innovation impediments, as the transatlantic economy accounts for nearly 50 percent of world GDP and 30 percent of world trade. The Final Report of the U.S.-EU High Level Working Group (HLWG) on Jobs and Growth raises several global issues for TTIP that are of interest to Intel.

First, the HLWG recommends that the U.S. and the EU reach bilateral agreement on globally relevant rules, principles or modes of cooperation on "localization barriers to trade." We strongly agree with this recommendation. Some governments are requiring businesses to locate R&D, IP and/or manufacturing within their borders as a condition of market access. If not contained, these emerging localization requirements will interfere with global supply chains that are essential to the ICT industry. They also will significantly impede the competitiveness of many EU and U.S. companies heavily dependent on emerging markets.

Second, the HLWG Report also recommends that the transatlantic negotiations address, among other items, "significant IPR issues of interest to *either* side" to "contribute to the progressive strengthening of the multilateral trading system." Again, we agree. The U.S. and EC negotiators already have discussed using TTIP to enhance trade secret protection by reflecting in the agreement the improvements they are making in their respective laws that protect this type of IP. In the information economy, the constant transfer of ever growing amounts of data on multiple digital devices enables trade secret theft to occur anywhere at any time. So, such theft needs to be appropriately deterred. The parties also should set global

---

[36] *See* Office of the U.S. Trade Representative, *Final Report of the U.S.-EU High Level Group on Jobs and Growth,* February 11, 2013.

principles on preventing forced technology transfer through broad compulsory licensing, disclosure of sensitive information as a condition of market access, or otherwise.

Third, the HLWG Report suggests that the parties enhance their "cooperation on conformity assessment and standardization issues globally." These challenges also should include curtailing the proliferation of unnecessary, prescriptive technology regulations that may be based on international standards. Such technology mandates are on the rise as more governments try to build up their local ICT infrastructure and industries, or overreact to legitimate privacy and security concerns.

Redundant and/or burdensome certification requirements also are troublesome, as they can delay or even block the entry of imports. Moreover, an increasing number of certification programs require unnecessary confidential business information that the receiving authority often is ill equipped to safeguard. Intel has provided other examples that impede innovation and trade in formal consultations with USTR and during stakeholder sessions at negotiation rounds.

If and when Congress considers Trade Promotion Authority, it should direct trade negotiators to fully address 21st century manufacturing challenges to help Americans prosper and create jobs at home.

V.   Employ a Combination of Mechanisms to Address Emerging NTBs

The world of trade is more complex than ever before. For example, we note that traditional non-tariff barriers such as local content requirements are (i) being expanded to require local data storage, design activities and intellectual property; and (ii) often are now combined with other barriers such as discriminatory incentives and domestic security initiatives that are counterproductive to both the local economy implementing them and global economic welfare. An assortment of trade tools is thus necessary to effectively tackle these complex behind-the-border measures.

At least three dozen countries have implemented national innovation strategies to increase their competitiveness and generate more economic growth.[37] The nature of those strategies differs widely among governments, however, and the difference between innovation and industrial policy is often murky at best.[38] U.S. companies increasingly face a host of measures intended to spur local R&D, IPR and manufacturing that are specifically exempt from WTO requirements, do not always comply with those requirements, and/or fall within the cracks of international restrictions on trade distortive measures.

One prime example of such measures is the proliferation of government procurement preferences in the BRIC countries that we mentioned in Section III.2. But there are others.

For example, a task force operating under the Indian Ministry of Corporate Affairs suggested several years ago that, as a bedrock principle of competition policy, intellectual

---

[37] Stephen Ezell, "America and the World: We're #40," *Democracy: A Journal of Ideas,* Issue # 14, Fall 2009, http://www.democracyjournal.org/article.php?ID=6703.

[38] *See generally* "The Good, The Bad and The Ugly (and The Self-Destructive) of Innovation Policy: A Policymakers Guide to Creating Effective Innovation Policy," The Information Technology and Innovation Foundation (October 2010).

property owned by a dominant company be made accessible to any third party that needs it to compete. On a related note, in 2010 a division in India's Ministry of Commerce argued that "compulsory licensing has a strong and persistent positive effect on domestic invention."

A number of the indigenous innovation policies that Indian regulatory authorities have been promulgating since early 2010 are very similar to those which the Chinese government has promulgated since 2005 and that the U.S. government is familiar with. For instance,

- As with the network regulations that the Certification and Accreditation Administration of China (CNCA) issued several years ago, in 2010 India's Department of Telecommunications required the disclosure of source code as part of its certification process.[39] The U.S. and other governments were able to persuade India, but not China, to remove that troublesome disclosure requirement.

- The Chinese government has supported an array of "voluntary" national standards that favor domestic technologies even when relevant international standards exist. Likewise, the Government of India is now supporting the development of Indian standards in the telecom sector.

The trend to pursue trade distorting innovation and manufacturing policies is not limited just to China and India, but is spreading to other regions.

Brazil, for example, is experimenting more deeply with industrial policy in the technology sector by providing incentives contingent on local production and investment.[40] The general legal framework for encouraging local R&D and manufacturing in Brazil has been in place for several decades, but recent implementing regulations on products such as tablets are micromanaging local content additions. Moreover, as in India, Brazilian policy linking incentives to local content is spreading to other regulatory areas such as spectrum allocation. Specifically, auction proposals by Brazil's agency over national telecommunications require a winning bidder to purchase an annually increasing percentage of locally manufactured and locally designed goods for the telecommunications and data networks that would use the spectrum being auctioned.[41]

Argentina has been targeting all imports by imposing ever more restrictive import licensing restrictions under which a license is not granted within the WTO required 60 day period unless affected companies meet unrelated government demands, such as agreeing to manufacture locally. Many U.S. companies still have products awaiting entry and are not making anticipated sales in the country.[42] Fortunately, a WTO panel recently ruled against at least some of Argentina's discriminatory measures and we hope this ruling will serve as a deterrent to other governments inclined to implement similar measures.

---

[39] *See* Template of the Agreement Between Telecom Service Provider and the Vendor of Equipment, Products and Services (28 July 2010).

[40] *See generally* Brazil's Information Technology Law, No. 8.248 (January 23, 1991)

[41] *See generally* ANATEL Proposal, Public Consultation No. 4 on the proposed tender rules for the 450 MHz and 2.5 GHz spectrum bands (February 2012).

[42] Multi-Trade Association Letter to Ambassador Ron Kirk and Deputy Assistant Michael Froman (February 10, 2012).

There is no single solution to solve these intertwined, complex and evolving trade distortive measures. Rather, the U.S. government should continue to employ a combination of mechanisms to convince governments to pursue a more open and proven approach to increase their competitiveness. To some extent, as noted below, the U.S. government already has been doing that with trade distortive regulations and policies that China has developed and enacted. Yet those existing mechanisms can be applied more robustly and to other emerging economies like India and Brazil, which also are working to develop policies that enhance their economies.

The following are some of the mechanisms that have shown to help address more fully the complex and evolving trade distortive measures.

1. Address Trade Issues Preemptively in Bilateral and Multilateral Fora

The Administration has had some success in working with China on a number of trade related issues in the U.S./China Joint Commission on Commerce and Trade (JCCT) and the more strategic or high level U.S./China Strategic and Economic Dialogue (S&ED). Through the JCCT the Chinese government has made many commitments, including the following:

- Stay out of royalty negotiations between IPR holders and let market forces govern,
- Improve IPR enforcement,
- Remain technology neutral regarding the standard or technologies used in 3G or successor networks,
- Delink government procurement from the origin of IPR,
- Cut back on information security certification rules that would bar a number of U.S. network products from the Chinese market so that they apply only to government procurement,
- Submit an improved GPA offer,
- Allow foreign stakeholders to participate in national standard setting activities as well as technical regulatory and conformity assessment developments,
- Provide a detailed account of its subsidies to the WTO by the end of 2005,
- Suspend indefinitely its proposed implementation of WAPI as a mandatory wireless encryption standard, and
- Eliminate its 70 percent local content requirement for wind powered equipment.[43]

A number of these JCCT commitments have been implemented. Others have not, or have been only partially implemented and often in a delayed manner. Still, as non-binding fora, the JCCT and S&ED have been very helpful because they allow and even encourage dialogue on general economic policies and specific trade issues (whether covered by trade rules or not) before they create significant damage to either economy. The Administration, however, may want to more carefully track the completion of the Chinese commitments made to date. In addition, the Administration may also want to apply a similar model to its U.S./India bilateral fora and the U.S./EU Transatlantic Economic Council, as those mechanisms do not seem to get the same attention or generate similar commitments from Indian or EU officials.

---

[43] See "China's JCCT Commitments, 2004-10," The US-China Business Council (As of December 16, 2010).

2. Establish Additional Best Practices and Principles Through Multilateral Fora

The development of international best practices, principles and standards can help fill in the "regulatory gaps" not suited for binding international agreements. These alternatives to national regulation have the unique benefits of being more flexible (e.g., not locking in technology), are easier to update, and ensure greater interoperability. Because of its non-binding nature, the Asia Pacific Economic Cooperation (APEC) has experimented extensively with principles and practices as guidelines to further enable the digital economy in its 21 member economies while balancing IPR, privacy, security, and other legitimate concerns.

For instance, APEC's Digital Prosperity Checklist ("DPCL") is "designed to assist APEC economies in promoting the use and development of ICTs as a means to enhance their ability to participate in the global digital economy." To that end, the DPCL "will provide a unique, yet critical tool for individual APEC economies to evaluate whether their domestic legal, regulatory, and trade policy frameworks are designed to positively impact the capacity of ICTs to generate value for their economies."[44] The DPCL references a number of ICT best practices and standards in connection with investment, infrastructure, innovation, intellectual capital, information flows, and integration of industries with the global economy. The DPCL best practices and standards developed with industry assistance serve as guides for national legislation where appropriate. As such, they should be reinforced by repeatedly referencing them in official documents and highlighting APEC economies that follow them.

There are various ways that the U.S. government could provide even more support than it already does for standards and best practices that address thorny trade issues not capable of adequately being solved through FTAs. Several examples follow.

A. Time Tested Innovation Principles

The drive by various governments to increase indigenous innovation makes sense as they seek to rise up the value chain and create more jobs within their countries. The challenge lies in crafting and implementing such policies so that they are both effective domestically and not trade distortive internationally.

The Administration and China agreed to develop some very high level time tested innovation principles to guide each government in developing policies that are not trade-distortive. The U.S. high tech industry then worked with USTR to develop some more robust innovation principles, which APEC adopted in November of 2011. Subsequently, the Administration wisely breathed more life into the APEC principles in the U.S./China JCCT held several weeks later:

> "Building on the innovation principles agreed to in the 2011 APEC Leaders' Declaration, China and the United States agree to use the JCCT Intellectual Property Rights Working Group to study investment, tax and other regulatory measures outside of government procurement, with the first phase of study in 2012 covering investment and tax, and the second phase in 2013 covering key measures in other areas, to determine whether the

---

[44] APEC Digital Prosperity Checklist (November 10, 2008).

receipt of government benefits is linked to where intellectual property is owned or developed, or to the licensing of technology by foreign investors to host country entities. The two sides will actively discuss removal of these barriers that distort trade and investment."[45]

The U.S. government should track adherence to the JCCT commitment and persuade APEC to monitor the implementation of the innovation principles among its 21 members. Otherwise, their benefit will be lost.

B. Global Cyber Security Standards and Best Practices

Industry and government have an equal incentive to ensure and increase information security, including cybersecurity.[46] Industry at large seeks a reliable and trustworthy cyber infrastructure that will encourage commercial activities and the continued growth of the global digital infrastructure. Governments want to (1) further extend cyberspace's benefits to their economies and citizens, and (2) prevent criminals from using cyberspace to undertake fraud, espionage, crime, and terrorist activities - activities that traditionally occurred offline.

Fortunately, governments, infrastructure owners, operators and users, and the information technology industry have a variety of tools to address information security and cybersecurity risks and challenges. These tools include technology standards, training, guidelines and best practices on information sharing, risk management, etc. As governments seeks to address risks in cyberspace, it is important that any measures they adopt properly reflect the borderless, global, interdependent cyber infrastructure. Internationally cohesive cybersecurity measures will promote interoperability, minimize "weak links" that result in vulnerabilities, lower costs for businesses that can deploy security measures globally, and free up vendors' resources to continue to invest and innovate. As noted in this Administration's Cyberspace Policy Review, "International norms are critical to establishing a secure and thriving digital infrastructure."[47]

Joint action from government and industry is necessary to address evolving security challenges in the global environment. They need to work together to develop policies and practices that take into account the dynamic and complex cyber environment, and quickly adapt to emerging technologies, business models, and threats. Divergent cybersecurity requirements adopted by countries without reliance on international policies and practices or technical assistance derived from a robust private/public partnership create uncertainty and inhibit the growth of e-commerce. For instance, the building of a telecommunications infrastructure in India slowed significantly in 2011 because that government, without an official consultation process, attempted to mandate contractual terms between telecommunications equipment vendors and Internet Service Providers for security reasons.

---

[45] See http://www.commerce.gov/news/fact-sheets/2011/11/21/22nd-us-china-joint-commission-commerce-and-trade-fact-sheet.

[46] The interdependent network of information system infrastructures that includes the Internet, telecommunications networks, computer systems, embedded processors and controllers, and digital information is collectively known as "cyberspace." Security enables this global digital infrastructure by creating a trusted, robust, and interoperable environment in which economic transactions and activities can occur.

[47] Cyberspace Policy Review: Assuring a Trusted and Resilient Information and Communications Infrastructure (June 26, 2010).

The "Encryption Regulation Best Practices" developed by the World Semiconductor Council (WSC) provide an excellent example of how private/public partnerships can tackle modern day cross-border issues effectively. Encryption is now ubiquitous in widely available ICT, including the semiconductors that Intel manufactures. For those widely available ICT products, the WSC best practices -- developed between 2009 and 2012[48] -- establish a presumption of no regulation except in narrow and justifiable circumstances (e.g., resulting out of international conventions such as export controls to prevent proliferation of munitions and weapons of mass destruction to targeted countries or targeted end users). To the extent that encryption regulation is necessary, the WSC best practices basically state that:

- Such regulation should not directly or indirectly favor specific technologies (including domestic algorithms), limit market access, or lead to forced transfer of intellectual property;

- The regulation should not mandate a specific technology because it will quickly become outdated, leading to less secure products;

- Any regulatory requirements must be applied on a non-discriminatory basis and respect intellectual property rights;

- Global collaboration and open markets for commercial encryption technologies should be strongly encouraged as both inherently promote more secure and innovative ICT products; and

- Any necessary licensing procedures should be transparent, predictable and consistent with international norms and practices.

These Encryption Regulation Best Practices were adopted by the six governments that have trade associations in the WSC. Those governments are China, South Korea, Taiwan, Europe, Japan and the United States, and they committed to promoting the practices to yet other governments. If promoted globally, the WSC best practices could prevent countries like Russia and India from enacting encryption regulation that could significantly impact the importation of U.S. IT products and reduce the security of domestic digital infrastructure by preventing leading edge products from being used.

C. Incorporate Best Practices into FTAs

USTR should consider using FTAs as a legal tool to push for, support, and even reference relevant international standards and best practices. For instance, in the information security space, among other initiatives based on private/public collaboration, FTAs could (i) rely on the common criteria assurance procedure where relevant; and (ii) incorporate emerging APEC work product "to develop options for effective cyber security initiatives against cyber threats,"[49] assuming those initiatives turn out to be feasible and well balanced.

---

[48] *See* Joint Statement of the 17th Meeting of the World Semiconductor Council, Lisbon Portugal, Annex 1: WSC Encryption Principles (23 May, 2013).
[49] Draft Okinawa Declaration, "ICT as an Engine for New Socio-economic Growth," The Eighth APEC Ministerial Meeting on the Telecommunications and Information Industry (TELMIN 8) (30-31 October, 2010, Okinawa, Japan).

Efforts to incorporate best practices into FTAs either as binding or hortatory language are not unprecedented. We understand the TPP agreement includes binding language that is based on the WSC best practices.

D. Find Ways to Establish "Living Agreements"

We must not only increase the pace of trade negotiations, but also ensure that the agreements being negotiated effectively address as many forms of emerging non-tariff barriers as possible. As Intel testified in a Senate hearing in 2010 on International Trade in the Digital Economy, there are a number of emerging trade barriers specific to IT goods and services that need to be addressed.[50] For example, much progress still needs to be made in liberalizing digital services. We are confident that similar gaps exist in other dynamic industries as product cycles continue to accelerate in time.[51]

USTR has improved and modernized the language FTAs over time. Of relevance to Intel, FTAs now enable e-commerce (as noted earlier); allow trade in both the equipment and devices that make up the IT infrastructure; and also allow trade in the digital goods and services the IT infrastructure enables. Moreover, the latest model language for FTAs contains various provisions requiring the Parties to cooperate on an ongoing basis; for example, to ensure regulatory alignment with international technology standards and prevent deceptive practices in e-commerce to enhance consumer welfare.[52] Such cooperative mechanisms are important to expand an FTA's capability to evolve as growth of the digital economy creates new challenges.

Another way to lengthen the useful life of an FTA is to include a periodic review mechanism where the negotiating parties commit to upgrade and expand the FTA. There is precedent for this in the FTA between Australia and New Zealand that is called Closer Economic Relations (CER). After initial adoption of the agreement's predecessor, there were several formal reviews every three or four years that resulted in additional provisions being added. The parties then decided to conduct annual reviews of CER, which is essential given how rapidly economies, business models, and technologies now evolve. A long list of additional agreements resulted from these annual reviews. One of the most important results of CER was the Protocol on the Acceleration of Free Trade in Goods, which resulted in the total elimination of tariffs or quantitative restrictions between the two countries. This agreement was finalized five years ahead of schedule.[53]

---

[50] *See generally* Prepared Statement of Intel Corporation, "International Trade in the Digital Economy," Subcommittee on International Trade, Customs, and Global Competitiveness, U.S. Senate (November 18, 2010).
[51] *See* "Forced Localization of Global Companies Business Activities," Handout given at The 2011 Global Services Summit: Engaging the Dynamic Asian Economies, Washington, DC (July 20, 2011).
[52] *See, e.g.*, KORUS Articles 9.4.1 & 15.5.2, 3.
[53] *See generally* http://www.newzealand.embassy.gov.au/wltn/CloseEconRel.html; http://en.wikipedia.org/wiki/Closer_Economic_Relations.

Conclusion

As Congress continues to explore ways to increase the competitiveness of U.S. industries, Intel recommends that it also work in parallel with the Administration to open up the biggest and fastest-growing emerging markets using a variety of mechanisms tailored to the issues at hand and to the targeted markets. These mechanisms should include mutually beneficial commitments on complex trade distortive issues derived from non-binding regular bilateral dialogues; the increase in and use of modern rules that take into account emerging non-tariff barriers; and the promotion of best practices and principles where FTAs do not reach the issues being addressed.

In sum, we need an increase in proactive standards, practices and binding international rules that are modernized to further reap the benefits of a digital economy. This recommended trade agenda is ambitious, but necessary to ensure America is in a position to effectively compete on a level playing field that benefits the entire global economy.

Response to a Question for the Record From Jacklyn Sturm
Senate Finance Committee Hearing
"The Role of Trade and Technology in 21st-Century Manufacturing"
July 17, 2014

Question from Senator Hatch

Question. Ms. Sturm, the TPP must be first and foremost about expanding trade opportunities for U.S. businesses and workers. I believe the TPP should only be concluded with those partners willing and able to meet the high ambitions of the agreement, including tariff elimination.

President Obama's lackluster approach to renewing Trade Promotion Authority, along with recent comments that he hopes to complete negotiations during his trip to Asia in November are starting to make me concerned about whether this Administration will do what it takes to get a good agreement.

Do you agree with me that substance needs to drive the timeline for completing the TPP negotiations?

Answer. Yes. Intel agrees that the quality of the substance, not an artificial deadline, should drive completion of the negotiations on the Trans-Pacific Partnership (TPP) Agreement. Many of the TPP parties are in the most dynamic economic region of the world. With a high TPP standard, this agreement will set a benchmark for other trade negotiations in the Asia-Pacific region. Moreover, some of the more settled and robust TPP provisions (for example, those addressing trade secret theft and unnecessary encryption regulation) already are being used as a substantive foundation or floor in the negotiations over the U.S.-E.U. Transatlantic Trade and Investment Partnership agreement. We should encourage our trade negotiators to continue pushing forward aggressively in securing significant new substance that will make the TPP a 21st-century agreement as originally contemplated.

Wyden Statement on Strengthening American Manufacturing through Fresh Trade Policy
As Prepared for Delivery

Americans – from the water cooler to professional societies – are often debating the future of American manufacturing. Academic journals are filled with articles where naysayers say that American manufacturers can't compete with cheap labor in Asia, or that robots and computers do the jobs once held by middle class workers.

This hearing will show that it is too soon to hang the crepe on American manufacturing, because there is reason to be optimistic. Many American manufacturing companies are succeeding in tough, global markets. Manufacturing accounts for more than $2 trillion of the American economy. It supports more than 17 million American jobs. And it drives three quarters of all private-sector spending on R&D. There are more players in the manufacturing game, but the bottom line is we're more than holding our own.

That's not to say that there haven't been significant challenges in recent years, and that it will be smooth sailing from here on out.

U.S. manufacturers have run up against greater competition today -- and some of it is unfair -- than in decades past. Fifty or sixty years ago, the United States was the world's factory, accounting for 40 percent of the world's manufactured goods. Today the U.S. accounts for less than 20 percent.

But American manufacturing has real strengths and opportunities to build upon. Technology is one area where America leads. The same is true in finished products and production methods. It is important for this committee to identify and examine which policies have stifled manufacturing and learn the lessons of the past. The focus today will be on fresh trade-related policies that can unleash the full potential of American manufacturers and give them a springboard to create good paying, middle class jobs.

There is a tremendous opportunity before American producers. There are about to be a billion new middle-class consumers in markets around the world with money to spend. And that number will only grow as more people rise out of poverty. Many of these consumers prize American-made products for their top-notch quality, safety, and reliability. The American brand sells.

Furthermore, America's manufacturers are at the forefront of the innovative fields that will lead our economy into the future – clean energy, health care, and information technology.

For example, Oregon's largest manufacturer, Intel, is here today. Their products are at the core of computing equipment and form the foundation of the global digital economy. Intel is competing and winning in tough global markets. And there are many more examples of vibrant manufacturers from my home state.

Brammo, based just outside Medford, makes award-winning electric vehicles. A-dec, based in Newberg, makes some of the world's best dental equipment. Erickson, based in Portland, makes heavy-lift aircraft for a huge number of uses.

There's no question that American manufacturing has a lot of room to grow. But I'm sure every member of this committee has seen thriving, cutting-edge manufacturers like these back in their home states. The investments these manufacturers make support healthy, stable communities, and they create good-paying jobs for middle-class Americans.

The right policies – especially on trade – can help kick off a new era defined by successful, sustained manufacturing in the U.S. Those policies should reflect what U.S. manufacturing looks like today and where it's headed in the future – not what it looked like 10 or 20 years ago.

They should dismantle trade barriers U.S. manufacturers face abroad – like tariffs on high-tech products, requirements to relocate factories, IP theft, and anti-competitive subsidies for state-owned enterprises. And they should foster an environment in which U.S. manufacturers of all sizes can grow and create good middle-class jobs.

The goal should be to make things here, add value to them here, and ship them somewhere. Today's hearing gives the Finance Committee a chance to develop trade policies that can help the U.S. meet that goal.

###

.